THE

BARROWFORD PRESS

≈ POCKET HISTORY SERIES ≈

Lower and Central
BARROWFORD

JOHN A CLAYTON

Published By
Barrowford Press

www.barrowfordpress.co.uk

2014

First published in 2009-2010 as the individual titles of:
Lower Barrowford, Central Barrowford

Introduction

The objective of this book is to trace the history of the township of Barrowford through the medium of the photographs left to us by our more enlightened forebears and the available historical resources. This will encompass large estates, farms, social life, cotton mills, economic highs and lows, times of celebration and times of tragedy.

The subject area covers the extended area within the modern boundaries of Barrowford. Within this extended district are the three sub-districts of Lower Barrowford (*Newbridge*), Central Barrowford and Higher Barrowford (*Higherford*). The following covers the first two of these smaller areas separately - beginning with **Lower Barrowford**.

This encompasses the separate districts of Reedyford, Newbridge and Newtown, Wheatley Lane Road, Laund, Carr, Noggarth and Rishton Thorns. The Newbridge area of the village is very much the product of the new factory system of the Victorian era when cotton spinning and weaving mills were erected, quickly followed by terraces of stone-built houses for the mill workers that now give the place its character.

That is not to say, however, that the history of Lower Barrowford dates only to the middle of the nineteenth century – far from it, in fact, as the farms and landed estates of the district will testify.

The course of the nineteenth century saw a marked change within the social and economic fortunes of Barrowford. The period of prosperity enjoyed by farmers and handloom weavers throughout the final decade of the eighteenth century proved to be fickle. Although the new industrial era brought wealth to a number of Barrowford people the nineteenth century also brought the downside of abject poverty to many others. Outside forces regulated both the supply of cotton to the voracious mills and the strength of the end market for their finished goods - many periods of sustained unemployment punctuated the better times of full employment through to the Second World War.

Lower Barrowford

Carr Mill Weir - water colour by Joseph Ogden

Reedyford

Reedyford seldom features within Barrowford history books and this is possibly because it is actually in the neighbouring town of Nelson! However, part of Reedyford was once considered to be a part of Barrowford and the close proximity of the two districts means that they have close historical ties.

In the fifteenth century the area of Whitefield, of which Reedyford was a part, came within the ownership of the Barrowford Bannister estate of Park Hill.

Reedyford House c.1910

It is not clear as to exactly when Reedyford House (sometimes given as Reedyford Hall) was built. In the early years of the eighteenth century a John Malham lived on the site and is recorded as having given the sum of £1: 13s: 4d in alms to a local charity from the income of his land at Reedyford known as The Poor Fields. The Hartley family owned the Reedyford site as part of their Bradley estate and in 1785 George Hartley, along with his two sons, William and Richard, built Reedyford Mill (or Hodge Bank Mill as it was commonly known).

Reedyford Mill Site

The mill stood beneath the spiralling elevated walk that now spans the M65, connecting Scotland Road v Reedyford Road. Among the partners in this new cot spinning venture were William and John Marriott Edge End in Marsden. The Marriotts were a Qua family with roots in the Kendal district; John wa highly gifted scholar accomplished in both the Latin a Greek languages and he also devoted a great deal of time to writing poetry. In 1788 John and William t over sole ownership of Reedyford Mill and, in 1795, J married Ann Wilson of Kendal who was a relative of famous explorer, Dr. David Livingstone. John died at age of 35 in 1798 and in that same year his one-year son, John, also died.

William Marriott then ran the mill with Henry Ecroyd and on William's death in 1806 the enterprise was leased to William Corlass and William Bolton. In the 1820s Corlass built some of the weaver's cottages fronting both the new turnpike road (now Gisburn Road) and the old Barrowford Lane (Corlass Street). Things did not go well for the partnership and Corlass went into insolvency in 1831. In September 1832 Reedyford Mill was offered for auction at the Kings Head, Colne with:

Closes of land, reservoir, dams, streams, falls of water, weirs, goits, water wheels, principal upright shaft, principal lying or tumbling shafts, engine house and chimney, gas pit, sizing house and chimney, retort house, firing house, purifying house and other appurtenances belonging; containing in the whole about seven acres and held by a term of years that will expire on the 25th March 1845. Rents together at £51:10s:0d. The water wheel is about 20hp and the premises are highly eligible for carrying on the business of cotton spinning. Immediate possession may be had.

William Tunstill

William Bolton lived in a farmhouse on the later Reedyford House site and took over the mill from Corlass, extending it in 1845. Robert and Abraham Clegg then took over the mill and ran it until it was purchased by William Tunstill who demolished it around 1870, the stone being used to build the houses on nearby Sandy Lane adjacent to the Steele Buildings (also known as 'Clock Cottages'). Tunstill had purchased 94 acres of land at Reedyford from the Bradley estate for which he was assessed, in 1873, at the sum of £554: 13s: 0d. It is probable that Tunstill had also demolished the Reedyford farm buildings around this time in order to erect Reedyford House.

By the time of its demolition the mill had been variously known as Newbridge Mill, Reedyford Mill, Boltons Mill, Cleggs Mill, Hodge House Mill and Hodge Bank Mill. Most of the workers throughout the history of the mill came from Barrowford and many were the stories attached to the factory. The mill had its own gas manufacturing plant and, in the early 1860s, the man in charge of the plant, one Sam Pickard, entered a disused gasometer with a lighted candle to inspect it and was crippled for life in the subsequent explosion.

William Tunstill built Reedyford House in the later nineteenth century and, alongside W F Ecroyd, he was the leading manufacturer of the district at this time. William and his brother, Robert, were from a family of blacksmiths from Wheatley Lane and they formed a limited company through which they erected and ran Bradley Mill in Nelson. William became a JP and a member of the Nelson Local Board, he was also a committed Wesleyan Methodist and it was partly through his influence that only a limited number of licenses were granted for the opening of public houses in Nelson.

Reedyford Brow

Reedyford House stood in isolation within enclosed wooded grounds. There were two entrances; one at the top of Reedyford Brow (on the Barrowford side of the canal bridge) with a gatehouse and the other facing what is now the Nelson and Colne College. A small gatehouse stood at the top entrance and a number of weaver's cottages clustered around the lower gate and across the road; there were around thirty cottages attached to the mill operation during the earlier nineteenth century. At the opening of the turnpike road (around 1806) a toll house was built opposite the top gate (roughly where the building stands in the photograph) in order to control the traffic from Nelson to Barrowford and Gisburn.

In 1888 it was formally announced that a new Primitive Methodist School and Chapel was to be erected at Newbridge at a cost of £2,800 but when the new building was opened on Maude Street in 1892 it actually cost £1,400 less than the original estimate. Jesse Blakey (author of the *Annals of Barrowford*) was appointed as Treasurer of the new venture and in 1904 two more vestries were added to house the 106 boys and 89 girls who were then in attendance. William Tunstill ploughed part of his manufacturing profits into the local Methodist movement, for which he acted as Treasurer, and he was involved in the running of the Trinity Chapel School standing almost directly across from the bottom gate to his Reedyford House estate.

William Tunstill died in 1903 and his son, Henry, inherited his estate. In 1911 Henry Tunstill of Reedyford House purchased a plot of land in the Pasture, at Barrowford, for £500 and donated it to St. Thomas' Church to enable an extension of the churchyard there. A memorial plaque to the Tunstill family was placed inside the church.

Reedyford Weslyan School (Trinity) c.1887

In 1915 Reedyford House was purchased by the Nelson Corporation and adapted to the use of an auxiliary military hospital. Following the end of WWI a fund was set up to enable the erection of a purpose-built hospital on the site and between 1918 and 1935 the local people raised a sum in excess of £20,000.

This was quite an achievement when it is considered that much of this sum was raised through the contributions of working people whose textile producing jobs were not always secure.

Many paid a few coppers from their wages each week and the proud new hospital (erected in 1935) stood as testament to the strong sense of community within the Nelson and Barrowford districts.

Reedyford House and Hospital

Between 1919 and 1935 the hospital at Reedyford was known as the War Memorial Hospital, the new building then became Reedyford Memorial Hospital. Prior to 1948 the hospital was a voluntary general hospital and, in 1948, it came under the wing of the new National Health Service as an acute hospital. In 1987 the site was cleared in order to make way for the new M65 motorway.

Roadworks on Scotland Road, outside the lower entrance to Reedyford House and above Reedyford Trinity Chapel

Nelson and Colne College – fire 1981

Nelson and Colne College was built on the open field site to the right of the roadworks in the early 1970s (the college caught fire in 1981 – photograph left). It would appear that the workmen (only one of whom appears to be doing any actual work!) are preparing the road for resurfacing, possibly in the 1930s. The lack of heavy machinery here is noticeable to the modern eye. The tram lines through Barrowford were finally stripped-out from the road sub-surface in the late 1960s.

The college engineering block occupied this site until its demolition in May 2009. This land was originally part of Reedyford Farm, within the Bradley estate, before it became part of the Tunstill estates of Reedyford and Carr Hall. The row of cottages behind the hay cart, and over the river, was built using the stone from Reedyford Mill following its demolition around 1870

Newbridge

The road bridge at Newbridge carries Gisburn Road from Barrowford to the middle of the River Calder where it then becomes Scotland Road, Nelson. This is not the exact site of the original river crossing ('*the reedy-ford*') as this was located fifty metres upstream from the bridge.

As the two townships of Marsden and Barrowford grew the ford was replaced by a wooden bridge. In 1787 there is a record in the Colne Church register referring to the bridge of that time as *The Cotton Mill Bridge* because of its close proximity to the new Reedyford Mill. On numerous occasions the bridge was washed away by floods and this led to long periods where travellers had to wade across. At these times men would carry women across piggy-back and this almost brought Tom Simpson to grief around 1840. A rather overweight woman required assistance and Tom, ever the gentleman, could not refuse. He managed to stagger half-way across the tumbling river when his strength failed causing the pair of them to take an unwanted swim. According to Tom they were lucky to escape with their lives and his wife dined out on this tale until her death when she was well into her nineties.

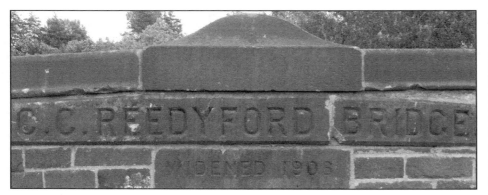

At the Preston Quarter Sessions of January 1838 the Blackburn Hundred made presentations to the court in respect of £1,000 to build a new permanent bridge at Barrowford. The old bridge (at Newbridge) was not of equal span and had been washed away by the recent flood of 28th December 1837. In the same flood one of the county bridges, erected in 1778, was washed down upon the estate of Mr Thomas Grimshaw esquire of Crow Trees. This latter was the Higherford Bridge and repairs were estimated at over £100.

A substantial bridge of double-span was eventually erected at Newbridge and this has served the people well. In 1803 the Marsden, Gisburn and Long Preston Turnpike Trust promoted the creation of a new road: . . . *from the canal bridge in Marsden to Walverden Water and the bridge intended to be built over the same and from thence to near the mill in possession of Mr. William Marriott and from the Methodist Meeting House to Pendle Water and the bridge over the same.*

This stretch of road was finally authorised in 1806 and in 1807 the two toll bars at Reedyford Brow and the George and Dragon were let for the sum of £286. The new road from Newbridge into Barrowford replaced the old Barrowford Lane that ran across land belonging to the Nutter family. This followed from the original crossing site along the riverside to what became Corlass Street (where the original road can still be followed), through the houses of Victoria Street and Harry Street, along the front of the old Berry's Victoria Mill, along the river at Old Row and behind the present shops to the Fleece Inn near the bottom of Church Street.

However, the creation of the turnpike road system was not without its problems. At the Lancaster Summer Assizes of 1867 the inhabitants of Barrowford Booth were indicted by the trustees of the Marsden, Gisburn and Long Preston Turnpike Road for non-repair of roads in the township. The road was said to have been in a bad state and a Bench warrant was issued against the Barrowford inhabitants in order for two of them to be apprehended, then let out on bail to appear at the next Assizes. This did little good, however - formal complaints regarding the roadway at Newbridge were made vociferously and often by the local people. In fact the road was so bad that carriage wheels became jammed in the deep ruts and the Nelson fire engine could take up to 30 minutes to arrive in Newbridge. This problem was finally addressed by the authorities in 1908 when the road was upgraded and the bridge widened.

Barrowford Old Road
A young Frank Birch on Corlass Street c.1930

This is the only remaining stretch of the original road through Barrowford. During the 'Dole Time' of 1863 unemployed men were put to work on civic schemes and it was at this time that a labour gang under the direction of Christopher Grimshaw, of Higherford Mill, erected the river wall that still runs from the bottom of Church Street to the Higherford Bridge. The stretch of road along Corlass Street was not walled until 1968 and this allowed the womenfolk of the neighbourhood to do their washing in the river. The riverside here was always busy on Monday morning wash-days when the weekly chore was combined with catching up on the latest gossip. This was a tradition that only really ceased around the time of WWII.

GISBURN ROAD BARROWFORD

This photograph was taken from the end of Roughlee Street around 1918 - the three old-timers on the form (extreme right) are sitting where the bus shelter is now situated. Looking up the length of Gisburn Road, towards Blacko Hill, this scene has changed very little in the past 90 years.

The row immediately to the right of picture was one of the first to be erected in Newbridge and was originally known as Spring Gardens owing to the fact that there was a large garden/allotment area to the rear which stretched back to the river. This garden site was eventually built over when Holmefield Mill was erected in 1907-8.

In 1861 there were 55 people living in the eight cottages of Spring Gardens row. In one cottage were the nine members of the Sellers family, six of them being weavers, probably at the nearby Reedyford Mill. The high proportion of working weavers within a single household meant that this family would have been relatively well-off. However, 1861 was the time when the American Civil War was beginning to impact on local trade and families such as the Sellers would soon feel the cold winds of change.

1967 flood

The two cottages at the far end of the Spring Gardens row are shown here (2nd and 3rd from right) during the Barrowford flood of 1967. These properties were occupied by Robert Bradshaw in 1855, one of them being the Spring Gardens beer shop. In 1841 Robert Bradshaw, a shoemaker aged 15, lived here with his widowed mother, brother and two sisters while his older brother, John, was a shoemaker at the opposite end of the row.

Robert learned to play the bass fiddle and joined the band at the Primitive Methodist Chapel, on Church Street; he apparently managed to reconcile his non-conformism with the liquor trade. In fact trade was so good in the expanding Newbridge district of Barrowford that Bradshaw was able to build the Victoria Hotel on part of the Spring Gardens next to his beer shop.

In 1861 there were eleven families living on Spring Gardens: these were Pickles, Sutcliffe, Driver, Thornton, Lonsdale, Holgate, Nowell, Whitaker, Rushton, Rycroft and John Blakey, a widower of 70, who was a shuttle maker and grandfather of Jesse Blakey.

Newbridge

At the end of this first row (adjacent to the second lamp standard) is 25 Gisburn Road. The cottages on this row were back-to-back with Grey Street and 25-27 were built by the Nowell family who farmed the Home Farm on Church Street. Grey Street was originally called Nowell Street.

The five cottages at the far end of the row (41-49 Gisburn Road - before Lee Street) were built in 1851 by the Ancient Order of Foresters on gardens that had been a part of the Bridge End Meadow. The Foresters was a Friendly Society through which members could take out loans and mortgages; the society had grown out of an earlier order of 'Royal Foresters' which was certainly in existence in 1790. At the end of 1886 there were a total of 540,441 Foresters in England. In the earlier days following their formation the Foresters' prayer entered into every ceremony of the Order but a curious feature was abolished in 1843. The Chief ranger presented new initiates with two cudgels and this would-be recruit was to appoint any Brother in the room as an antagonist. They then engaged in combat at the close of which the sub-chief ranger reported that *The courage of the candidate has been fairly tried according to the ancient custom and he is found worthy.* It was then explained to the initiate that as Adam had to fight and contend with wild and savage beasts in the forest so had all faithful Foresters to contend *With the world, the flesh, and the Devil.*

Clock Cottages

Along with Spring Gardens this was one of the very first rows of cottages to be built in the Newbridge district. In 1837 a tailor by the name of John Steel purchased a plot of land (at £30:12s:0d) in the Bridge End Meadow belonging to the Sutcliffe family on which he built the cottages. The modern photograph (right) shows the original frontage of the houses along which Sandy Lane ran (between the houses and the river) up to Wheatley Lane. The clock was installed for the benefit of the workers at Reedyford Mill and the tenant of the cottage was paid one shilling per week to wind it up.

John Steel (1802-1856), and his wife, Ellen (1801-1855) had a house at Newbridge in the early nineteenth century rated at £8:4s:6d and they also owned cottages at Reedyford Bridge near to the Trinity Chapel. In 1837 Steel also bought land in a field called Pastures on which he built Victoria House. This property fronted the main road and stood adjacent to Foulds Street (on what is now the MUGA site below Rushton Street School). In 1881 the house was occupied by another tailor called William Tattersall, along with his son Starkie who was also a tailor. This property was nicknamed 'Cabbage House' because it was said that Steel 'cabbaged' cloth (charged for pieces not used) when making suits - the Clock Cottages were also known as 'Cabbage Row' for the same reason. Tattersall began tailoring at Victoria Houses in 1837 and the property remained a tailor's premises until at least 1930.

The Empire Picture Palace

The Barrowford Empire Picture Palace, to give it its Sunday title, opened on Nora Street in 1913. The cinema was also known as the Empire, The Empire Palace, Palace Pictures, Newbridge Cinema and the 'Penny Scratch.'

William Taylor was the managing director and he promoted variety shows alongside the latest cinema releases. In February 1927 the lessee of the cinema was Betty Gableton, the house manager was Douglas Milton, reserve manager was Cyril Bell and his assistant was Bert Holgate. By the following year Charles Gaston had become the general manager and in 1930 the lease had been taken over by William Hargreaves, his general manager being Wilson Stobbart. Two years later (1932) the picture house projectors flickered for the final time.

The Electricity to power the lights and cine projector of the Empire was obtained by stringing power lines across the gardens at the back of the building and over Grey Street where they were hooked up to one of the electricity stanchions on the main road that supplied the trams. Following closure the building eventually became the Empire Garage and then the Popular Garage (the name it still carries today). The photograph shows the building as it is now - the original decorative facade was removed many years ago. During the 1920s and 1930s films were also shown on most Saturday afternoons in the upstairs assembly room of the Central Co-operative building near to the bottom of Church Street.

*Lower Clough Mill
Lower Shed and Engine House*

The Barrowford Room and Power Company purchased a three acre plot of land known as Lower Holme from the owners of Lower Clough Farm on which they contracted the local building firm of Messrs. Boothman and Company to erect their new mill. Opened in 1891 the Lower Clough Mill was intended to house a number of smaller manufacturers who would rent the floor space and steam power provided by the Room and Power Company.

The main manufacturer within the factory was Christopher Atkinson who moved from the neighbouring Calder Vale Shed and Victoria Mill in Nelson, to take up most of the space in the new Lower Clough enterprise. Atkinson lived in the large semi-detached house of Willow Bank on Wheatley Lane Road, near to the top of Sandy Lane. The partnership of Wilson and Hartley also took space at Lower Clough where they ran about 200 looms. The main body of the mill was built on three floors with 22 windows on the length running along Wilkinson Street. Behind this was the shed, with a capacity of well in excess of 1,200 looms, and the warehouse.

Things went well for the Power Company, for a few months at least, but on the 6th January 1892 the new edifice came crashing to the ground. During the day the engine tenter had noticed that one of the engine bearings was running hot and, at 6.15 pm, he decided to stop it in order to let the mechanic have a look at the problem. As things turned out this was to be a fortunate event as the lack of power meant that the mill workers who were reliant on machinery had to call it a day and go home. Around 8 pm two men were working on warps in the twisting room but neither of them noticed that one of the healds, hanging from its frame, had been placed too close to a wall-mounted gas light. Within minutes the room became an inferno and there was nothing to be done other than call the Nelson Fire Brigade.

The Brigade arrived some 30 minutes later, delayed by the poor state of the roads, and immediately their pride and joy was brought into action. This was the gleaming steam pump they had acquired in 1873 and had named the *Lord Nelson*. The three cylinders of the Shand Mason engine were capable of pumping 600 gallons of water per minute and the main hose was soon firing a strong jet of water from the river weir into the bowels of the raging building. Unfortunately the delay in tackling the fire, coupled with a strong wind that joyously fanned the flames, meant that little could be done other than to save the engine house and lower weaving shed.

Lower Clough Mill
Wilkinson Street

The gutted warehouse had contained Atkinson's stock valued at £9,000 and the damage to the building was estimated to be not less than £12,000. Fortunately the premises and their contents were fully insured and the building was quickly rebuilt on a single level. In January 1960 Pioneer Weston Ltd., (Pioneer Oil Seals) of Cotton Tree, took over the mill and ran it until 1976. The mill is now occupied by several smaller firms.

Calder Vale Shed

The Barrowford Co-operative Manufacturing Company bought a plot of the Bridge End Meadow, between the Clock Cottages and Lower Clough Mill, with the intention of building a mill for their members. Unfortunately the scheme never came to fruition and, in 1867, the Company sold the land in two separate tranches to former business partners Abraham Robinson and James Atkinson.

Robinson was a stone mason and built the Calder Vale Shed in 1868 while Atkinson, a joiner, built a saw mill on his part of the land. John Sutcliffe and Barnard Atkinson were the first tenants in the new mill and nine years later the partnership was dissolved. Atkinson carried on until 1885 when his son, Christopher, took over the business and, by this time, the building had been extended. Christopher Atkinson and Company moved to the newly built Lower Clough Mill in 1891. From this date Calder Vale Mill was occupied by a number of small manufacturers, the last being Vale Weavers Limited, of Nelson, who worked the mill until its closure in 2005. The site is now (Summer 2009) undergoing development for housing.

The Oddfellows Hall

The building here stands on the corner of Garnett Street and Sandy Lane to the south-east of what was the Calder Vale Saw Mill yard. This surviving testament to the working men's movement now houses a couple of small enterprises and its silent facade belies the drama of over a century of social interaction.

The *Order of Oddfellows* grew out of a necessity for the working people to insure themselves against the vagaries of life when there were no trade unions, National Health Service or welfare state to see them through the difficult periods when disease and unemployment struck.

In the eighteenth century many skilled and semi-skilled Lancashire craftsmen were excluded from access to trades guilds because the scattering of small towns here meant that there were not enough people of any particular trade to organise such enterprises. The only real alternative to poverty was the self-help afforded by craftsmen from an odd assortment of trades combining within a single guild and hence the *Guilds of Odd Fellows* came into being. Over time the Oddfellows Guilds became Friendly Societies dedicated to the mutual welfare of their members through financial benefit.

The *Loyal King William the Fourth Lodge of Oddfellows* was founded in 1830 but it is unclear as to where they met until they took the Sandy Lane building at Newbridge. They appear to have been here by the middle to later period of the nineteenth century and, by all accounts, the Lodge was a successful one. In 1879 John Tate was Secretary of the Newbridge Lodge which had around 180 members. However, by 1884 the increasing wealth of the working members of the Lodge meant that their payment of a few shillings per week as insurance against poverty was beginning to seem increasingly unnecessary. In the following year a majority of members proposed that the Lodge be wound up and the proceeds shared amongst themselves. The Oddfellows Unity Valuer stated that the Newbridge Lodge held approximately £5,500 in capital and property – this translated to a payment of £30:18s:0d for the 178 qualifying members. Much to the chagrin of the wider Society of Oddfellows the final decision was made to wind up the King William the Fourth Lodge in June 1886.

This would certainly not be the end of the social aspect of this building as the *Royal Antediluvian Order of Buffaloes* were based here for a number of years. The RAOB, or 'Buffs,' operated as a working men's club well into the later part of the twentieth century. The initiation certificate (right) for this Lodge was presented to George Proctor, of Hill Farm, Briercliffe, in February 1933.

Lower Clough Farm

The Lower Clough Farm buildings stand on Pendle Street and have been converted into two neat semi-detached houses. A good number of the properties in Newbridge were built on the land belonging to Lower Clough Farm; the estate extended from Wheatley Lane down to Calder Vale. As we have seen, Lower Clough Mill was erected on Lower Clough land from where it took its name.

The Reedyford, Carr Hall and Newbridge districts are low-lying lands that would always have been highly susceptible to flooding. This explains the high number of 'holme' and 'carr' field names, both of which signify wet riverside ground. It would appear that the land around Newbridge in particular suffered from being waterlogged because the area was once known as Mire Hole. Lower Clough Farm was also known as Mire Hole Farm while Calder Vale was often referred to as Mire Hole Mill; there were also two Mire Hole Cottages nearby. It would not be until the eighteenth century that serious efforts were made to drain the Newbridge holme fields and this is when the majority of the farms, such as Lower Clough and Lower Laithe, became established.

In 1841 Lower Clough was farmed by John Harrison (aged 45), his wife, Betty (50) and their household servant, Ellen Judson (14). It is not clear as to the size of the farm at this time but an estate map of 1847 shows that there were just over 20 acres belonging to Lower Clough. By 1861 John Brown (58) was farming 15 acres at Lower Clough assisted by his wife, Margaret (53), son John (17) and daughter Margaret (14). Others in the family were daughter Martha (11), Sarah (6) and Alice Cutler (78 - widowed).

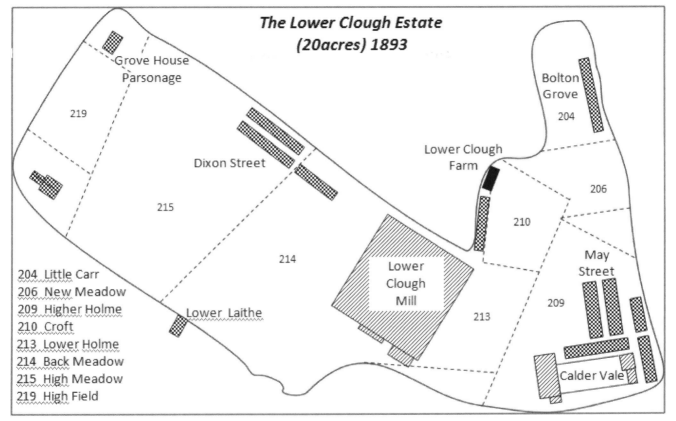

The Lower Clough Estate (20acres) 1893

Grove House
Parsonage

219

Bolton
Grove

204

Dixon Street

215

Lower Clough
Farm

206

210

214

Lower Clough
Mill

May
Street

209

213

Lower Laithe

Calder Vale

204 Little Carr
206 New Meadow
209 Higher Holme
210 Croft
213 Lower Holme
214 Back Meadow
215 High Meadow
219 High Field

By the early years of the 1890s Newbridge was beginning to develop in response to the increasing demand for workers in the new mills. From this point onwards there would be an unprecedented growth of new houses around Barrowford but nowhere would develop to the extent of Newbridge

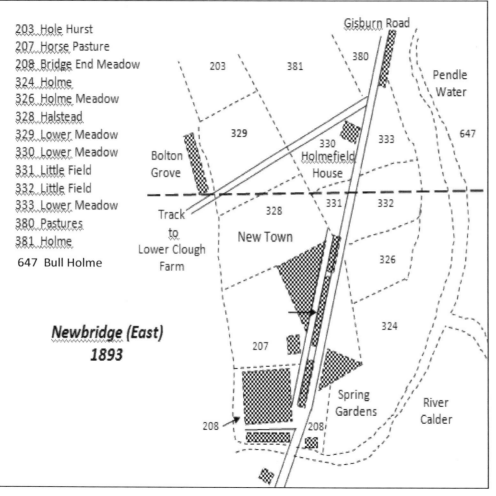

203 Hole Hurst
207 Horse Pasture
208 Bridge End Meadow
324 Holme
326 Holme Meadow
328 Halstead
329 Lower Meadow
330 Lower Meadow
331 Little Field
332 Little Field
333 Lower Meadow
380 Pastures
381 Holme

647 Bull Holme

Newbridge (East) 1893

Gisburn Road

203   381   380

Pendle Water

329

Bolton Grove

330 Holmefield House   333   647

Track to Lower Clough Farm   328   331   332

New Town

326

207   324

208   Spring Gardens

208   River Calder

The plan (left) shows the extent of development in Newbridge (east) between the Clough Farm estate and the river and south of a line drawn through Mount Street to Bull Holme

In 1871 John Brown was farming 22 acres at Mire Hole Farm along with his wife, three daughters and a servant boy named Francis Hargreaves. Also living at Mire Hole Farm was John's son, John (a stonemason), who had married a girl name Jane from Slipper Hill Farm in Blacko.

By 1881 William Haythornthwaite (46), who had earlier moved over to Higham from Easington in Yorkshire, was farming at Lower Clough with his wife, Sarah (43), daughter, Mary (12), son Henry Garnett (7) and daughter, Hannah (5). The middle name of Garnett given to young Henry

Haythornthwaite would suggest that his mother, Sarah, was related to the Garnett family of Barrowford after whom the Newbridge properties of Garnett Street were named.

The 1991 census returns show that William Bleazard (66) was now farming Lower Clough. William, along with his wife, Mary Ann (64) originated in Bolton-by-Bowland before moving to Grindleton, where their son, James (now 33) was born, and then taking a farm at Brierfield where their daughter Sarah (now 27) arrived on the scene.

John Dixon

Dixon Street was built on the High and Back meadows of Lower Clough Farm, above Lower Clough Mill. John Dixon was a manufacturer at Lower Clough Mill, Walverden Shed and Holmefield Mill and it is thanks to his foresight and generosity that Barrowford has been able to enjoy the park that has played an integral part within the village for over eighty years. On 18th May, 1922, John Dixon donated the land for Barrowford Park (Mill Holme and Coney Garth) to the Urban District Council. On the same day Samuel Holden gave the Bull Holme for the creation of the recreation ground. Together at 15 acres the lands were bought by Holden and Dixon when Lower Park Hill Farm came up for sale. The purchase price was £3,125 and a further 17 acres were purchased by public subscription at a cost of £1,325. Work commenced and the mill leat from the lodge to the old mill was filled in and made into a footpath in June 1925.

Dixon Street

In June 1895 John Bowler of Barrowford (builder) and Robert Stansfield (joiner) purchased land from the estate of Jonathan Stansfield (who built Blacko Tower) to build part of Garnett Street - namely numbers 32 to 44 - on land formerly owned by Lower Clough Farm. Bowler and Stansfield were in direct competition with William Boothman and Company, the Nelson firm of builders who had erected Lower Clough Mill. However, the competition was somewhat one-sided with regard to Lower Clough land - the Boothman firm won most of the contractual work because William Boothman had married Mary Wilkinson who was co-heiress to the Lower Clough Farm lands. Boothman and Company went on to build the rest of Garnett Street along with many other properties in the area.

Mary Wilkinson was the daughter of Henry Wilkinson and Mary Garnett (who had married in 1829) and were the owners of the Lower Clough estate. A Wilkinson family legend has it that Mary's family arrived in Barrowford having fled the Jacobite Rebellion. The Garnett family were related to Oddie Sutcliffe, the wealthy farmer who owned the Bank Hall estate (now the Lamb Club) - Wilkinson Street and Garnett Street were named after the Lower Clough family.

During the period between 1890 and 1920 Newbridge was a permanent building site; so quickly were the green fields evolving into rows of stone-built terraced houses that the area became known as New Town. A few major builders were responsible for the erection of the new houses, shops and workshops - chief among them being James Atkinson, the Bowlers, Boothman and Company, Thomas Duerden and Lot Lee. This latter built much of Lee Street and, in 1906, Thomas Duerden, joiner, builder and funeral director, of number 3 Joseph Street, gained planning permission to erect nine houses on May Street.

The Bowlers were a family of bricklayers who moved from the Midlands to Barrowford in order to take advantage of the building boom. The head of the family was John Bowler who, in 1891, lived at 101 Gisburn Road with his wife and sons. Moses Bowler lived at 17 Garnett Street, Richard Bowler was at Back Joseph Street and another John was at 17 Joseph Street. It is likely that the family built most of the properties in which they lived. They built a lot of the houses at the lower end of Nora Street and Gisburn Road; on the 22nd of November 1929 the representatives of Emmanuel Thomas Preston, a carriage proprietor of Nora Street, sold to Norman Bowler, of 63 Castle Street, Nelson: *'all that plot of land including 2, 4, 6, 8, 10 and 12 Nora Street'* for the sum of £600.

Holmefield House

Most of the terraced rows in Newbridge were named after the family members of the people who commissioned the properties and so we see the Berry girls of Holmefield House commemorated in Lucy Street, Maude Street and Ann Street.

Sam Holden

The brothers Samuel and James Holden might have been the last men to build a new textile mill in Barrowford but they were certainly not the least. Sam Holden worked for Christopher Atkinson at Lower Clough Mill until 1899 when he left to join his brother James in business at Walverden Mill. Before long the brothers were running 305 looms at Seedhill Mill and, in 1907, were able to set up the Holmefield Mills Company. Their new Holmefield Mill was erected in that same year by James Atkinson on the riverside Holme in Barrowford, the other partners in the venture being J. Shackleton and W. H. Atkinson.

Holmefield opened in August 1908 with 2,100 looms, the space being divided into four to accommodate the Holden brothers and three other tenants. In 1910 the Stow Brothers, who had formerly worked the 'old mill in the park,' were working 520 looms, the Holdens ran 640, William Brown and Company had 560 while John Dixon ran 400. In 1915 Holmefield became the first commercial property to be hooked up to the new electricity power lines.

Holmefield Mills
The chimney viewed from Bull Holme

The steam engine at Holmefield was a 1,000 ihp horizontal cross-compound built by Cole, Marchent and Morley in 1907. This type of engine was designed to economise through provision of a high degree of superheat in the steam but unfortunately there was a payback in the fact that lubricants of the day were unable to cope with the heat. The Holmefield engine required three rebores and two replacements of the high-pressure cylinder over its lifetime

James Holden had retired by 1920 and this left Sam as the principal partner. By the middle of the 1920s a third brother, John Brown Holden, had become a salesman and junior partner of the Holmefield Company. John had started the business of the Roughlee Laundry in Roughlee Mill and Sam Holden built the Roughlee Laundry building behind the Sunday school, overlooking the river at Newbridge and this gave its name to Roughlee Street. This was one of only a very few streets in Barrowford without any house frontages - Occupation Street (leading to Corlass Street) and Wilkinson Street spring to mind as other examples.

By 1935 the other tenants had vacated Holmefield and the private company of Samuel Holden Limited had been set up with 1,700 looms weaving shirtings, furnishing fabrics and rayon dress goods. By now the firm had established itself as the largest manufacturer in the village with around 800 workers. Sam Holden's, or Sam's as Homefield was widely known, had started life many decades after the old established Barrowford firms such as the Berrys and the Barrowcloughs but the modern principals upon which the firm was built and operated meant that it managed to survive until the industry became almost untenable.

Sam Holden died in 1942 and control of the company passed to his daughters and sons-in-law, Rex Mayall and Arthur Hindley. Sam's only son, Ernest Airlie, was killed in the First World War. In the mid-1950s the firm became part of Hindley Brothers who were taken over in 1964 by Carrington Dewhurst (later Carrington Viyella). In 1968 the row of shops and houses on Gisburn Road called Forest View, formerly used as offices for the mill, were demolished and a new warehouse was erected on the site in 1969. In the following year 1,000 looms were producing shirtings, rainwear, trouser fabrics and crepe bandages as Carrington Menswear Manufacturing. As the 1980s dawned redundancies began to bite when 300 workers lost their jobs. In 1995 more lay-offs were announced and by the following year the mill ceased to operate. The site was quickly absorbed into the ever hungry maw of housing redevelopment and only the two date stones now remind people of the many thousands of jobs created over some eighty years for the workers of Barrowford and the surrounding district.

Sam Holden's football team c.1910

The Dixon Street Murder

On the 26th of February, 1897, events that had been simmering within a terraced house on Dixon Street finally came to a head and the tragic events that were played out here shook the quiet village of Barrowford to its foundations.

In the late afternoon of that fateful day Sarah Ann Nowell, and her cousin-in-law, Constance Nowell, sat at the kitchen table quietly finishing their tea of boiled ham and discussing the events of the day. As Constance arose from the table to clear the dishes the man of the house arrived home and let himself in through the back door. Without speaking a word Fred Nowell, the husband of Sarah Ann, carefully closed the door, placed his heavy winter overcoat on the hook fastened to the back of the door and turned the key in the lock.

He then made his way over to the kitchen sink where he poured himself a glass of water and, having taken no more than a sip he put the glass in the sink then fumbled in the deep side-pocket of his coat. He slowly withdrew a shining, metallic object and swung the hand that held the object behind his back so as to hide it from the view of the two women. All the while Connie had been watching her cousin Fred and turned to Sarah with

WANTED
FOR WILFUL MURDER

FREDERICK (FRED) NOWELL

WHO DID FELONIOUSLY, WILFULLY AND WITH MALICE AFORETHOUGHT MURDER HIS WIFE IN THE LANCASHIRE TOWNSHIP OF BARROWFORD ON THE 26TH DAY OF FEBRUARY IN THIS YEAR OF 1897

DESCRIPTION: AGED 34, HEIGHT FIVE FEET FIVE OR SIX. MEDIUM BUILD. LIGHT SANDY HAIR BALDING. COMPLEXION FRESH, EYES BLUE-GREY. NO WHISKERS OR MOUSTACHE BUT MAY BE WEARING FALSE MOUSTACHE. DRESSED IN BLACK SERGE REEFER JACKET AND VEST, DARK BROWN CHECK TWEED TROUSERS, LOW SHOES, TURNED DOWN COLLAR AND FRONT, BLACK AND GREEN WOOL DRESS TIE. WAS LAST SEEN WITHOUT HAT. HE HAD ABOUT £20 IN HIS POSSESSION, AND WILL PROBABLY ENDEAVOUR TO EMIGRATE.

Lancashire Constabulary Head Division, Preston

a quizzical look and a shrug. The ladies of the household had been used to Fred's odd behaviour but he now appeared to be behaving in a more peculiar manner than was usual even for him.

Finally he turned and spoke to his wife, who was still seated at the table. His voice was a pitch higher than normal and Sarah noticed the beads of sweat on his forehead in spite of the cold that the day had brought.
"Report me did you then?"
Sarah glanced across at Connie, unsure what to say to her husband.
"Well, you won't get the better of me!"

By now his voice had risen almost to a scream. He brought his hand round from where he had been concealing its contents and Connie saw the bright flash of polished steel. Fred Nowell raised the shining new Kinnoch .360 calibre pistol and pulled the trigger. Sarah saw an instant flash of yellow flame emerge from the barrel but she never heard the deafening crack of her husband's first shot. Neither was she aware of having been violently thrown backwards from her chair as the black powder cartridge spat a soft-nosed lead bullet deep into her brain.

The Kynoch .360 revolver

In a state of semi-consciousness Sarah's survival instincts were screaming for her to make an exit from the family house that had suddenly become hell. She crawled towards the front door, finger nails scrabbling desperately at the linoleum floor covering in the passage-way. At the same time Nowell had turned his attention to Connie who was begging him not to shoot again. Her plea fell on deaf ears; as he raised the revolver and aimed at his cousin's face Connie put her hand out in an automatic reaction to save herself. The first shot rang out sending a bullet through the flesh and bone of Connie's outstretched hand and into her jaw. The gun cracked again and another bullet hit the shattered hand quickly followed by another that entered the hapless victim's shoulder, spattering a perfect arc of blood across the whitewashed kitchen wall.

Having maimed his cousin, Nowell then turned his attention back to his wife. He walked slowly and deliberately into the front passage-way where she lay bleeding heavily and gasping for life. Sarah was unaware of her husband as he strode over her comatose body; breathing deeply he puffed out his chest and, revelling in the avenging power that he now wielded, aimed the revolver for the final time and fired a bullet into the back of his helpless victim's neck.

Sarah Ann Nowell

In the meantime Connie was trapped; she could not escape the house through the locked back door and the front exit was blocked by her murderous cousin. In desperation she took the only way out – with the adrenalin coursing through her veins Connie swung her clenched fist at the kitchen window and was relieved to see it shatter. Climbing out into the cool welcoming air she did not feel the deep lacerations of the jagged glass slicing into her flesh; she had lost all sense of reality and survival was the only thing driving her now. Leaving a trail of blood along the stone flags Connie ran to her neighbour, Mrs Brown, two doors down the hill and raised the alarm.

As Mrs Brown ran into Back Dixon Street she saw Fred Nowell emerge from his yard; he was agitated and hesitant – he looked frantically up and down the back street before making up his mind which way to make his escape. Without overcoat or cap the fugitive squeezed through the iron railings at the top of the back

street and ran upwards through the field in the direction of his employer, Christopher Atkinson's home at Willow Bank. This was the last that was ever seen of Fred Nowell in his native village of Barrowford.

To understand the tragic events of 1897 it is necessary to travel back to the early 1860s when we first see Fred and Sarah making their mark on the Victorian world. Frederick Nowell was born in February 1861 at Flax Moor Farm in Blacko. He was the illegitimate son of Susannah Nowell whose father, James, had farmed at Old Laund and New House (Blacko) before taking over Flax Moor. By the time that Fred's grandfather, Joseph, arrived at New House Farm he was describing himself as a cattle dealer and his two sons would follow him into the profession.

Joseph died in 1868 and his son, James, took over Flax Moor while Fred moved with his mother and grandmother to live at Poplar Cottage (16 Back New Road Side) in Barrowford. Also living here were Fred's uncle Thomas and his wife, Elizabeth. By 1881 Thomas, a successful commercial traveller, had moved to the Eccles district of Manchester where he and Elizabeth had six children, all under ten years of age.

In 1879 Fred's mother, Susannah, married Hartley Wilkinson who described himself at that time as a farmer from Middop. Hartley was born in Barnoldswick in 1831, the son of a grocer, and had worked his way up through the textile trade until he eventually had a lucky break when his sister married William Wilkinson, a Barrowford man who owned Pendle Street Mill in Nelson. Hartley Wilkinson became a partner in the business and moved his new wife, and step-son Fred, to live at Rimington.

The 1880s was to prove to be an eventful decade for the Nowell family. Fred's uncle, Richard Nowell, passed out of his training as a dentist and chemist in Manchester and set himself up in business at 137 Gisburn Road. This is the shop fronting the main road at the bottom of the front car park of the White Bear Inn – this property was to remain as a chemists shop almost until the present day. Fred's grandmother died, both his uncles, James and Peter, went bankrupt as cattle dealers, Fred's mother Susannah died, Fred married Sarah Ann and his Uncle Thomas' wife, Elizabeth, died in Eccles leaving him with seven young children to raise alone.

Sarah Ann Davis was born in 1865 at a place called The Lyndon, a small, quiet district of the Staffordshire iron-working district of Wednesbury. The daughter of proud parents, John and Emma Davis, Sarah was soon to have a baby sister, Fanny. The girls grew up in a happy, chapel-going Methodist society and Sarah Ann won a prize at the age of twelve when she was chosen by the National Methodist Council for her services to the church.

Wednesbury
Sarah Ann's birthplace

As the girls entered their teens the economy in South Staffordshire slowed and, at the tender age of thirteen, sister Fanny found herself being sent northward to work as a domestic servant for the Duckett family at number 28 Accrington Road in Burnley. Alfred Duckett was a director of the much respected Burnley building firm of James Duckett and Sons - the company had been started by Alfred's father, James. As a youngster James had joined his brother as an apprentice stone mason and they worked together on the erection of Barrowford St. Thomas' church between 1837 and 1841. However, the Duckett name soon became synonymous with sanitary ware; their goods, such as the *Duckett Clencher Toilet Bowl*, were shipped around the world.

In 1883 Sarah Ann followed her sister north when she became a domestic help to a Barrowford family; she settled well in the village and became a valued member of the Wesleyan community. It is probable that Sarah and Fred Nowell met within the mutual social circle of Sarah's employer and Fred's step-father. Whatever the case might have been Sarah and Fred were married on Saturday the 7th of January 1888 at St. Thomas' Church. The bridesmaid was Sarah's sister, Fanny, and the best man was Fred Nowell's friend, James Bleazard from Lower Clough Farm.

Fred Nowell (seated left)

This photograph was supplied to the Nelson Leader following Sarah Ann's shooting. It is possible that it was taken at the time of Fred and Sarah's wedding in January 1888 and this would suggest that the other two men were James Bleazard (standing) and the Rev. A F S Studdy.

Before their marriage Nowell stated to Sarah that the matrimonial home would need to be one where there were doors to the front and rear as he could not bear to live in a house with a single door. Nevertheless the newlyweds moved into a back-to-back property with a single door and Sarah began to notice that her new husband's behaviour became distinctly odd. This was the beginning of the loveless marriage that Sarah had to endure for almost ten years before her husband finally brought a violent end to it.

The year following Sarah's wedding her sister, still living with the Duckett family, fell gravely ill with typhoid fever and, despite the best efforts of the medical profession she passed away at 2.30pm on the 26th of October, 1889. She was just twenty-four years of age. The sisters' parents having died many years ago Sarah now found herself without any blood family and with a violent, psychopathic husband whose unfounded jealousy would culminate in the natural conclusion of his final act.

By 1891 Fred was working as a clothlooker for Christopher Atkinson at Lower Clough Mill and he moved with Sarah into Joseph Street. With money from his mother's estate Fred also purchased two houses on nearby Duckworth Street. Around 1893 the couple moved up the hill to live on Dixon Street and events took another turn. Fred's Uncle Thomas buckled under the strain of raising his young family single-handed and in the year that the Nowells moved into Dixon Street he died at the age of forty-two. The decision was made for three of his orphaned children, Constance (the eldest at eighteen), Susannah (thirteen) and Margaret (eleven) to move in with Sarah and Fred. To a certain extent this took some of the pressure off Sarah as, for a while at least, her husband curbed his violent outbreaks. This was not to last, however, and as the years slipped by Nowell increasingly accused Sarah of having an affair with any man she spoke to.

Fred Nowell

The violence increased until Sarah could see that her life was now in danger. Finally she plucked up the courage to report her husband to the Police and they encouraged her take out an Order against him. On the afternoon of the shooting (26th February 1897) Sarah and Connie had been to Colne to take out an injunction but Fred, disguised in false whiskers, had followed them. This act of defiance by his wife outraged him and he took himself off to Burnley where he purchased a new revolver, drew out his life savings of £20 and returned home to carry out his evil deed.

Following his escape Fred Nowell made his way in the darkness over Middop Moor to Gisburn where he purchased a new hat and other clothing from Nancy Robinson at the Park View Post Office and Millinery Stores. The Gisburn police, in the form of Constable George Firth, were informed of Nowell's escape by Superintendent Barnett of the Nelson force. However, Nowell made it to Hellifield where he was recognised by a local farmer who knew the Nowell family but the evidence begins to cloud from the point of his buying an express train ticket at Hellifield Station. Some reports say that the fugitive caught the train to Carlisle while others state that the ticket was never handed in at any onward station and was, therefore, never used. There is no hard evidence to show that Fred Nowell ever left the shores of Britain; he certainly would not have used his own name when registering with an outbound ship. However, the fact that he was obsessed with the New World, especially Australia, would suggest that emigration would be his intention. If he had indeed used his ticket to Carlisle then it would be a simple matter for him to take the connecting train to Glasgow from where a great number of passenger ships plied their trade with the New World.

As for those Fred Nowell left behind . . . Sarah slipped into a coma and died at home a few days after the shooting. Over £100 was raised by the people of Barrowford for Connie who was maimed for life – understandably not wishing to remain in the Dixon Street property she took a house in nearby May Street where she lived quietly with her brothers and sisters until her death some twenty years later. Connie was buried in the same grave as Sarah Ann at Wheatley Lane Methodist Chapel.[1]

---

[1] The full story of the Dixon Street murder is the basis of a historical novel: Clayton. J. A. *Cotton and Cold Blood.* Barrowford Press (2008)

Trough Laithe

Trough Laithe Farm now stands a short distance to the south of Wheatley Lane Road as it climbs from the Clough up to its highest point at Gough Nook. An estate map of 1847 shows that the narrow trackway that now leads from Wheatley Lane Road to the farm was once the main road. In fact the length of Wheatley Lane Road, from St. Thomas' church to the All Souls Catholic cemetery, was widened and altered in its course during the early part of the twentieth century.

The name of *'laithe'* strongly suggests a date for the building of Trough Laithe Farm within the eighteenth century. The style of building, where one or more cottages were incorporated with a barn (in a single structure) was common during the period 1720-1800. *Laithe* originally applied to a barn, especially an out-barn, but the type of farm building seen at Trough Laithe had assumed the name of *laithe house* by the end of the seventeenth century.

At some period during the later 1700s it would appear that Trough Laithe was purchased by the owners of the Park Hill estate. Certainly by the early 1800s the farm was listed as Park Hill property with land at 100 acres – an 1847 estate map, however, shows there to have been some 37 acres attached to Trough Laithe. It would appear, then, that as the farm was bounded by the lands of Carr Hall, Parrock Farm, Carr Hall, Laund, Sand Hall, Higher and Lower Fulshaw, Clough and Lower Clough one or other of these neighbouring estates (probably Carr Hall) had absorbed over 60 acres of Trough Laithe land before 1847.

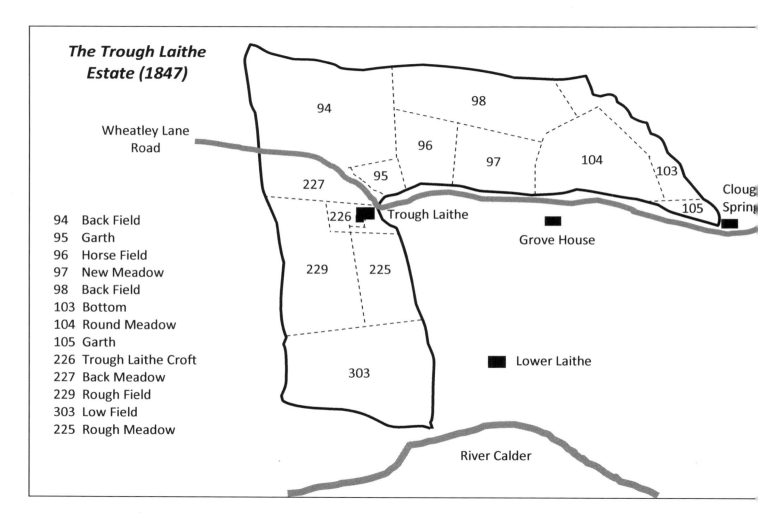

The Trough Laithe Estate (1847)

Wheatley Lane Road

94   Back Field
95   Garth
96   Horse Field
97   New Meadow
98   Back Field
103   Bottom
104   Round Meadow
105   Garth
226   Trough Laithe Croft
227   Back Meadow
229   Rough Field
303   Low Field
225   Rough Meadow

94
98
96
95
97
104
103
227
226   Trough Laithe
105
Clough Spring
Grove House
229
225
303
Lower Laithe
River Calder

In 1841 Mary Bolton, a widow (aged 75) was farming at Trough Laithe along with her two unmarried daughters, Mary (30) and Jane (25). It is possible that Mary was born at Trough Laithe as the census record shows her to have been born at Wheatley Lane Road. She married a Bolton and in all likelihood her husband would have been from the family of John Bolton who lived at Hubby Causeway, where the lodge for Oaklands House now stands. The Boltons were a well known family around Barrowford from the early nineteenth century to at least the middle of the twentieth century.

Helping the Bolton women out at Trough Laithe in 1841 was Luke Brown who lived-in at the farm and was described as an agricultural labourer. By the 1850s Luke's brother, John Brown, was working the farm alongside his business as a part-time property auctioneer. Brown was responsible for selling many farms around the district during the later nineteenth century, an example being an auction he carried out in September 1857 for the sale of the Hubby Causeway buildings and land. Particulars for the auction were to be had from Mr Stephen Wilson's house (the George and Dragon) or from Mr Ingham Walton of Bank House. Here it was stated that one of the fields, named Hole Hurst, would be suitable for the erection of a mansion house. This, however, was not to be and in the early 1950s the Council estates of Oaklands Avenue and Higher Causeway were built on this land.

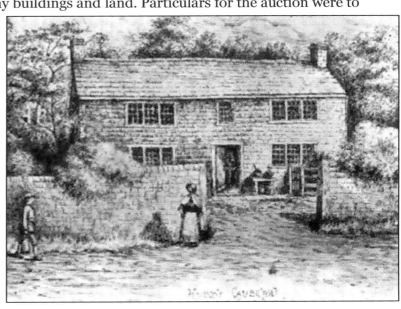

The Hubby

John Brown was still farming and auctioneering in 1861 when the census shows him at Trough Laithe with his wife, Elizabeth, who was formerly called Harrison and, like her husband, was born

Trough Laithe Barn

in Colne. With them were Elizabeth's daughter, Mary Ann Harrison (27) a cotton weaver, and John and Elizabeth's children (all born in Barrowford) - Nicholas (22) a weaver, Robert (18) a blacksmith, Elizabeth (15) a weaver, Richard (13) a farm worker, Luke (10) a scholar, Sarah (8) a scholar, John (5) a scholar and Emily (1).

The next census returns for Trough Laithe (1871) show that John and Elizabeth Brown are still at the farm. John is now 55 years of age and Elizabeth is 57 – it appears that John is no longer an auctioneer as he is described as a 'farmer of 36 acres' (this is the same area shown on the 1847 estate map). With them are children Richard, Luke, Sarah, John and Emily along with John's grandson, Albert Brown (13) a farm servant.

By 1881 John Brown had died and Elizabeth is shown as the head of family at Trough Laithe and is described as an annuitant. Still with Elizabeth are son Richard, an indoor farm worker, daughter Sarah who has by now married a Stuttard from the family who farmed neighbouring Lower Laithe, and her daughter (Elizabeth's granddaughter)Emily (3). George Fell (36), of the family who ran the Fleece Inn, was an indoor farm servant (a farm labourer who lived in). Also living at Trough Laithe in 1881 are John and Elizabeth's youngest daughter, Emily, and her husband Ezra Bolton (27), a tin plate worker, with their son Harry Bolton (1). Ezra was the son of John and grandson of the first John Bolton of Hubby Causeway - the Bolton family had returned to Trough Laithe after an absence of some 40 years.

By 1885 a William Pickles was farming at Trough Laithe and he was still there in 1896. The farm was converted to housing in the later twentieth century.

Quarrying in the 18th century

Mention the word 'Noggarth' to most Barrowford people and they will immediately associate the name with the quarry. This photograph was presented to me as a photograph of workers at Noggarth quarry in the later part of the nineteenth century. The sandstone quarry at Noggarth has been long abandoned but its angled face of bare rock still remains as testament to the days when demand for a massive increase in housing for the influx of textile workers to the district led to a 'gold rush' of suitable building material sites.

Noggarth quarry fell within the Sand Hole Farm estate (later known as Sandy Hall) and the name of the farm provides a clue as to why the quarry was sited at that particular spot. In the later Medieval period, when an increase in demand for new agricultural land led, in turn, to an increase in demand for manure, the material that was the easiest to come by for this purpose was *marl*. Thousands of tons of this gritty sand were used locally to improve the new intake of former waste land into agricultural land. This is borne out by the large number of sand-related names in the district - Sand Hole, Sandy Lane, Sandy Ford etc., were almost exclusively sites where marl was extracted, in many cases leaving gaping holes in the landscape. And such was the case at Noggarth where marl extraction led to the winning of sandstone on the same site which, in turn, formed the quarry at Noggarth as we see it now.

Noggarth Quarry (2009)

The sand and marl layers could be up to five metres in depth locally - men were paid one penny per day to dig the material so the pits they left behind were known as *'penny holes.'* A number of these pits existed around Sand Hole, one immediately to rear of the farm became a quarry and another one could be found to the north of Wheatley Lane Road, in fact this is still known as Marls Hill. Beside marl and stone there were also surface coal winnings around Noggarth, the largest being in the Coal Pit Field next to the main quarry.

The northern boundary of the Sand Hole/Noggarth estate also forms the parish boundary between Roughlee and Barrowford. At the corner of Hay Seed Field, once a part of the smallholding at Noggarth Top (see plan opposite), the parish boundary heads south and then west where it encloses the area of Rishton Thorns. This is a detached portion of Barrowford that was originally common land within Pendle Forest granted to the half-dozen or so farmers of Barrowford as part of their tenancy rights. These rights remained until the early sixteenth century when deforestation took place and Rishton Thorns was split between the Spencer and Inn farms. These two farms were owned in 1566 by Richard Towneley. Although the small district of Rishton Thorns has been historically a part of Barrowford the people from there have always maintained their independence as 'Wheatley Laners.'

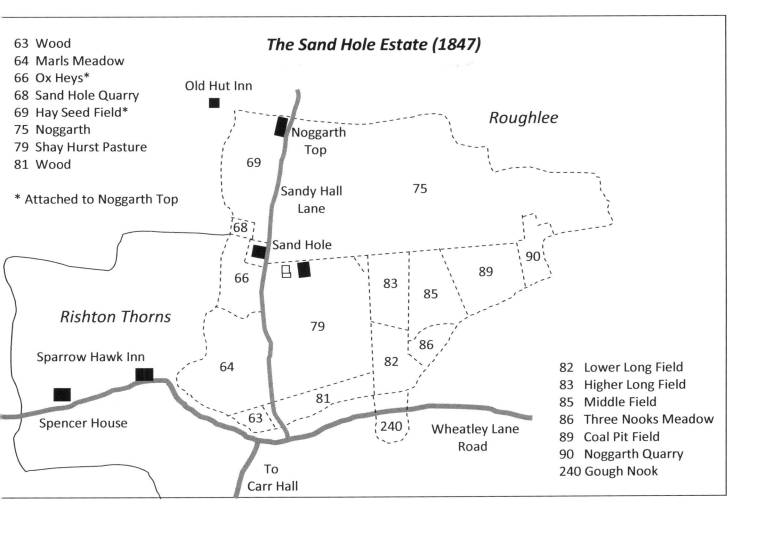

The Sand Hole Estate (1847)

63 Wood
64 Marls Meadow
66 Ox Heys*
68 Sand Hole Quarry
69 Hay Seed Field*
75 Noggarth
79 Shay Hurst Pasture
81 Wood

* Attached to Noggarth Top

Old Hut Inn

Roughlee

Noggarth Top

69

Sandy Hall Lane

75

68

Sand Hole

66

90

89

83

85

79

Rishton Thorns

Sparrow Hawk Inn

Spencer House

64

82

86

81

63

240

Wheatley Lane Road

To Carr Hall

82 Lower Long Field
83 Higher Long Field
85 Middle Field
86 Three Nooks Meadow
89 Coal Pit Field
90 Noggarth Quarry
240 Gough Nook

Noggarth Top Cottage

For many years Noggarth Top has been a small shop-cum-cafe serving the many walkers who have ventured out from the smoke of the industrial valley in search of the fresh air and superb scenery of the Pendle Forest.

It is possible that the cottage was originally built to house the workers who quarried for coal, marl and stone in the Noggarth area. It could equally well occupy the site of a sixteenth/seventeenth century squatter's dwelling (a smallholding erected without official permission); the Clitheroe overlords, who owned the land, commonly turned a blind eye to this practice as the rent for the house and newly cultivated land was welcomed. Until the later 1870s Noggarth Top had 22 acres of land attached and this might serve to bolster the argument for the property having originally been an unofficial smallholding.

The cottage was used by successive families for handloom weaving and this would supplement the income they gleaned from the attached land. By the time of the 1881 census returns Noggarth Top Farm, as it was described, was uninhabited. The smallholding was no longer viable as handloom weaving was not an option; 22 acres would not support a family and the only viable alternative for those who once lived here was to move down the hill and take a job in one of the mills in Nelson or Barrowford.

In 1841 the Shaw family lived at Noggarth Top where the head of the household, John (35) was a cotton weaver. John lived with his wife Isabella (25), sister Jane (35) and children Thomas (10), Abraham (7), George (6), Nanny (2) and an unnamed daughter of 3 days. It is probable that the family were handloom weaving and running the smallholding at this time.

Twenty years later the 1861 census illustrates the trend towards the factory system where William Witham was head of family at Noggarth Top. William (47) is a 'cotton power loom weaver' while his wife Harriett (43) is a cotton spinner, an occupation into which daughter Margaret (15) had followed. Another daughter, Elizabeth Ann (10) was a scholar.

The land attached to Noggarth Top Farm appears to have been taken over by a neighbouring farm by 1871 as we see Mary Gill, a laundress (44) living at the cottage with her children, Catherine (14) and Florence (13) who were both weavers along with Maud Mary (5) and Angelina (3). By 1881, as we have seen, the cottage was unoccupied.

Sandy Hall Lane
Between Noggarth Top and Sandy Hall

Sandy Hall Lane is an ancient trackway running directly to the front of Noggarth Top and down the hill to Sandy Hall. The lane was a late Medieval route along which the people of Barley, Newchurch, Dimpenley, Wheatley Carr and Roughlee travelled with their corn to be ground at the King's Corn Mill at Bradley.

The track was also used to carry woven cloth pieces from the handlooms of the outlying districts to the merchants in Marsden, Barrowford and Colne. In modern times the route connected Pendle Forest with the industrial districts of Nelson until the Noggarth Top Road was upgraded, thus rendering Sandy Hall Lane obsolete to all but local farmers and walkers. There is also a possibility that the trackway is far more ancient than this given the fact that it connects with the truly ancient ridgeway route running from Ribchester, along Noggarth to Ridgealing and onwards to Yorkshire. These inter-ridgeway routes often have their origins within the depths of our pre-history.

Sandy Hall

It is unclear from the census information given in the 1841 returns as to who was farming the Sand Hole estate. This early census is somewhat skimpy on information and we can only guess that the head of household was Alice Cutler (55) who lived with her son William (13) a cotton weaver, daughter Alice Smith (30), and granddaughter Samuel Smith (10). Also in residence were another family, James Jackson (55), described as a hawker, and his wife Anne Jackson (55). It is, of course, possible that Alice Cutler and daughter Alice Smith ran the farm with the aid of outside labour. James Jackson, as a hawker, would have been a trader or retailer of some description – possibly delivering coal, stone or farm produce by cart to the outlying districts.

Haytime at Noggarth

This photograph was taken in 1927 and illustrates a period in modern times when work in the mills was in short supply. On the far left is Harold Birch, of Victoria Street in Barrowford, and third from the left is his neighbour, Stephen ('Stivvy') Stow, a well known pigeon fancier of Corlass Street.

Both of these men were weavers in Barrowford who, finding themselves on short-time work, were eking out their meagre wages by helping to gather the hay crop on a local farm. The other two men are not known but the one second from left appears to be the farmer, possibly Mr. Lancaster of Ridgealing. The roof of the barn at Sandy Hall can just be made out above the wall in the far right centre of the photograph. In the background is the height of Kings Causeway in Nelson while a steam train heads from Nelson to Brierfield in the valley. Noggarth quarry is one field distant behind the group.

In 1861 Sand Hole Farm extended to 66 acres and was being farmed by John Rhodes (53) with his wife Elizabeth (35),who was a local girl from Roughlee, and their offspring James (13) a farmer's labourer, Mary Ann (11) a scholar, Robert (9) and Isabella (1).

The 1871 returns provide an insight into the reasons why Noggarth Top Farm ceased to be a smallholding. John Rhodes and his family were still the main farmers at Sand Hole but also there are Luke Cutler (34), a farmer of 20 acres, his wife Sarah (29), born in Newsholme, and sons John (2) and Harry (11 months). The fact that Luke Cutler had been born around 1837 means that he should have shown up on the 1841 census at Sand Hole. The fact that this was not the case indicates that Luke was not living here at the time of the census and could well have been away from home, perhaps only for a night or two, with his father.

This would mean that Alice's husband would have been the farmer at Sand Hole. Luke is farming 20 acres at Sand Hole in 1871 and this is almost certainly the land that was formerly attached to Noggarth Top thus confirming the earlier suggestion that this property was no longer a farm by then.

In 1881 we see that John Rhodes and his family still occupy Sand Hole where all of them now appear to have been working on the farm.

Sandy Hall from Sandy Hall Lane

The Sand Hole area formed part of the fourteenth century vaccary (cattle farming) system of Lower Barrowford but there is a suggestion in the name of *Noggarth* that this area was farmed at a time before the Normans arrived. The Old English translation of *garth* is *enclosure* while *nog* can be taken as either *north, walled* or *abundant* – any of which could be used as a qualifier prefixed to *garth*. The 16 acre field of Noggarth (field number 75) was developed as the Pendle Forest Golf Club between the wars but was eventually abandoned in favour of the Marsden Golf Course. The Pendle Club House stood on Sandy Hall Lane, opposite to, and a little way above Sandy Hall.

During the eighteenth century the higher slopes of the Noggarth Field were used as a meeting place for the villages around Pendle. The military held a number of gatherings here where the local army officers would stir up the crowds of local people in the hope of getting them to enlist. However, more often than not these recruitment drives would end in mayhem as the locals threw stones at the military and beat the officers.

All Souls

In a corner of the Lower Long Field, on the former Sand Hole estate (fronting onto Wheatley Lane Road), stands the All Souls Catholic cemetery. In the later part of the nineteenth century this land had been purchased by Alexander Bell. The cemetery plot was purchased from Bell (a partner in the Hartley and Bell Clough Springs Brewery who lived at Wheatley

Lane) in 1897 for the sum of £300 - the foundation stone for the small mortuary chapel (now demolished) was laid by Bishop Bilsborough in 1900. The first interment took place on Good Friday in 1901 and the chapel and cemetery were officially consecrated by Bishop Casertelli in 1906.

The total cost of works at the new cemetery, including the land, fencing, draining, building the chapel and erecting the entrance came to £900 which was raised by providing shares at £150 to each of six local parishes. The ornamental gates forming the entrance to All Souls were taken from the hall that became the Brierfield Town Hall, once owned by Robert Tunstill – the brother of William Tunstill of Reedyford House.

Directly opposite the All Souls cemetery gates is the narrow lane leading down to Laund Farm. At the top of the lane, on the Fence side and fronting Wheatley Lane Road, stood a barn belonging to the Laund Farm. On the first OS survey map (1840s) this barn is shown as the Sparrow Hawk Inn while the Sparrow Hawk Inn as it is today was described as the Rishton Thorns Inn. In the *Annals of Barrowford* the author, Jesse Blakey, made a number of enquiries of local people in the 1920s as to why the Laund barn was marked as an Inn and, finding no evidence for this, he finally came to the conclusion that the map was wrong. Two houses now occupy the site of the barn.

The Old Sparrow Hawk Inn

The hamlet of Rishton Thorns centred around the Sparrow Hawk and nearby Spencer House.

Although the Inghamite Chapel is in this immediate vicinity it is, technically, outside of the Rishton Thorns boundary. In 1841 the Inn was occupied by Robert Hargreaves (60) who was born in Old Laund, his wife Ann (65), son Joseph (35) and daughters Louisa and Jane (both ages rounded to 30). Ten years later Robert Spencer (75), born in Wheatley Lane, is the head of the family at the Inn where he is described as an Innkeeper and farmer of 38 acres. Robert is still an Innkeeper at the Sparrow Hawk in 1861, by now he is a widower of 88 years living with his daughters Lucy (55), Jane (51) and Martha (26), all housekeepers, along with Edward Thornton (39) also a widower and a manservant at the Inn.

The Inn is being run by Alexander Riley (54), born in Colne, in 1881 but he is living at Spencer Farm with his wife Margaret (48 née Exley) of Foulridge, daughter Ann (8), Richard Pratt (53) servant and Margaret's uncle, Robert Exley (67), a gardener.

Laund Farm is situated mid-way along a steep trackway that led from Marsden, over the River Calder and up to Wheatley Lane Road. As we have seen there was a barn at the top of the lane, on the Fence side, and on the Barrowford side of the lane is a detached house that was once the Laund Cafe. This business catered for the many walkers and cyclists who passed this way during the 1950s and 1960s. A carved stone is embedded within the wall of this property, fronting the main road. This was a boundary marker showing the division of two estates in relation to who was responsible for the upkeep of the road. The carved **EC** denotes Every-Clayton (Carr Hall) and, according to the *Annals of Barrowford*, **JH** stands for John Holt. However, it is probable that the intials are those of James Hargreaves of Laund.

There is one name that can be said to have been truly synonymous with Laund and that is Hargreaves. The oldest remaining building here is the late sixteenth century house built very much in the standard architectural style of other houses in Barrowford by the emerging yeomanry of the Elizabethan period. The house would have replaced an earlier timber-framed farm house of around the fifteenth century - surrounded by land granted to the tenant as part of the estate of the lords of Clitheroe. Going back some 250 years before this the Laund was an integral part of the Clitheroe hunting district of Pendle Forest where the deer were allowed free grazing within a clearing, or park. The Laund here (Barrowford) is not to be confused with the other areas of Pendle Forest with the same name i.e., Old Laund, New Laund, Higher Laund etc.

Laund Farm and Houses c.1910

During the seventeenth century the Hargreaves family were farmers at Barrowford Water Meetings from where they built a substantial estate through dealing in woollens and money-lending. It is probable that James Hargreaves, of Water Meetings Farm, built the White Bear Inn and his eldest son, John, inherited the Water Meetings estate. John's son, also John (born 1684), married into the family who lived at Laund and went to live there. John was widowed and inherited the property, he then married his cousin, Catherine (born 1709) who moved into Laund. By the middle of the eighteenth century the Laund estate was owned by James Hargreaves who was described in the diary of Elizabeth Shackleton, of Pasture House in Barrowford, as her husband's 'pot companion.' In 1774 Elizabeth's diary observes that; *'I rode out over the new road on White Moor. Mr. Shackleton was happy with his pot companion, old Hargreaves of the Laund, who came quite drunk from Colne and made a noise as was abominable - too rude to describe.'* The diary is also scathing about James Hargreaves' son, Abraham, who is described as *'idle and a wastrel.'* James died in 1791 and Abraham went on to set up Barrowford Mill (in the park) as a spinning enterprise and his own diary makes fascinating reading.

The Elizabethan house at Laund was upgraded by the Hargreaves family who removed the west wing and attached a Georgian house to it. Jesse Blakey was of the opinion that this did nothing for the aesthetic appeal of the old house which is now overshadowed by its new close neighbour.

Laund House

The last Hargreaves to occupy Laund was James, a qualified solicitor who never actually practised. Hargreaves lived the life of a country squire but unfortunately he was somewhat unhinged. In 1905 Sarah Jane Haythornthwaite took the position of housekeeper at Laund only to find

herself being beaten by her employer. When the matter came before the court Sarah Jane was awarded damages of £400 and the judge was of the opinion that Hargreaves was 'quite out of his mind.' The same thing happened to a subsequent housekeeper, Henrietta Appleyard, who was awarded £100 in 1914. Hargreaves decided to move to Manchester after this; later he moved to Blackpool and it was here that things took a turn for the worse. A writ was to be served on Hargreaves for some reason and the solicitor responsible sent his secretary, Frank Hinchcliffe, to serve the writ on Hargreaves at his house in Osborne Road, South Shore. As Hinchcliffe entered the house Hargreaves fired a revolver at him and he was struck in the abdomen. The victim was taken to hospital in a critical state but died soon afterwards - Hargreaves was arrested. The court recognised that he was insane and sentenced him to life; during his sentence in Broadmoor he became known as the fattest prisoner within the whole of the British Isles before dying in prison in 1936. James Hargreaves was buried at St. Thomas' church and he left a legacy of £50,000 to Nelson Corporation to pay for the setting up of a rifle shooting range. Understandably the Corporation considered this to inappropriate!

The Remains of Laund Farm (2010)

All that remains of the farm now is the ruin of the end cottage. There were originally two cottages attached to a barn in the style of an eighteenth century laithe house. The trackway through the Laund site is still a footpath, one end of which now exits onto the Barrowford-Padiham bypass while another branch cuts across to Carr Hall Road, this once connected Laund with Parrock and the Carr Hall estate.

The Laund Estate (1847)

87 Marl Pit Field
91 Marl Pasture
93 Sate Mouth Field
99 Collings Clough Field
100 Noggarth Meadow
226 Dole Field
230 Humphrey Field
232 Laund Croft

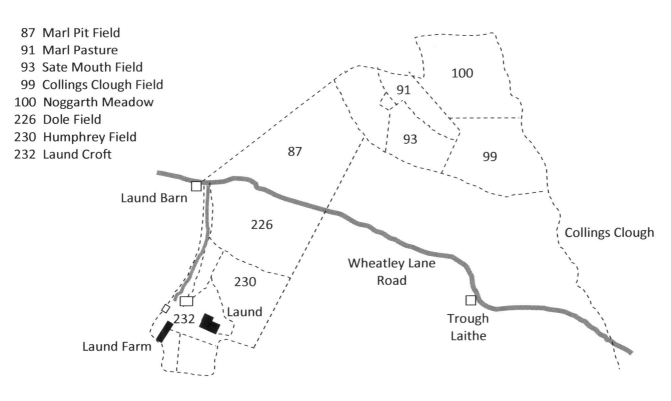

100

91

93

99

87

Laund Barn

226

Collings Clough

Wheatley Lane
Road

230

Laund

232

Trough
Laithe

Laund Farm

In 1847 the Laund estate ran to some 25 acres although it would originally have been bigger than this. Over time the neighbouring Carr Hall estate absorbed Laund land and it would appear that this was added to Higher and Lower Parrock Farms. The Sate Mouth Field would probably have been an area where a spring or field drain emerged while the Humphrey Field would be named after a Humphrey Hartley who farmed Laund in the sixteenth century.

There were a number of separate dwelling on the Laund estate but living in the main house in 1841 were Ann Hargreaves (80), her son James (35), Sarah (40 - a relative) and James Dickinson (20). All of these were described as being of independent means. Also at the house was Maria Blakey (14) a household servant. At the farm were two families by the name of Dean the head of one family being Jane (45) along with her 11 children – two of these were agricultural labourers on the farm while a third was a corn miller at Carr Mill.

In another dwelling were Richard Hargreaves (25) a cotton weaver, and Ann Hartley (2). John Aldersley (40) was an agricultural labourer and lived at Laund with his wife Sarah (35) and five children while another Dean family were headed by Richard (20) a shuttle Maker, his wife Margaret (20) and daughter Elizabeth (11 months). In yet another dwelling we find John Broughton (40) a cotton weaver.

Hargreaves' Laund House

In 1861 we find at the main house bachelor James Hargreaves (56), of whom Elizabeth Shackleton was so scathing. James is shown as a land and house proprietor and is living with Rebecca Dyson (78), a widowed housekeeper and Henry Dyson (19) who is a cotton stripper and grinder – Henry is described on the census as James Hargreaves' grandson but he could be the grandson of Rebecca Dyson. Mary Ann Ashworth (16) is a household servant.

Elizabeth Harrison (72), who was born at Stonedge in Blacko, lives next door in the old house along with her niece Margaret Judson (12). George Hartley is the bachelor farmer of 23 acres at Laund and is assisted by his brother, farm hand Dan Sharp (53). Hartley's sister Olive Sharp (56), of Blacko, is a housekeeper. In the other farm cottage lives James Aldersley (35), a railway porter at Nelson Station, with his wife Mary (34) and Mary Moore (71), a housekeeper.

By 1871 James and Mary Aldersley have taken over the farm of 23 acres. Robert Stuttard (39), a shoemaker from Gisburn, is next door with his wife Sarah (32) and four children. In the main house we find Sarah Hargreaves (36) a widow and an 'owner of property' with her children Ann (7) and James (1), both of whom are also described as 'owners of property.' As we have seen this James was to die in Broadmoor at the age of 66. Servants in the Hargreaves household were Mary Slater (19) and Sarah Wilkinson (14).

In 1881 the main Hargreaves family are either not at home on census night or they have moved out of Laund for the time being. Servants at the main house are bachelor Robert Hargreaves (51), a coachman and Ann Wilkinson (25) his half-cousin and dressmaker. The Crompton family live in another dwelling (probably the old house) where Mary (40) lives with her daughter Mary (3), servant Jane Stiley (15) and coachman James Jennings (43) from Ireland. Hartley Halstead (38) is running the farm, which has now reduced to 19 acres, with his wife Ellen (32) and their children Margaret Ann (7), Nancy (3) and Martha (11 months). Hartley is still farming at Laund in 1896 while James and Mary Aldersley have moved to the neighbouring farm of Higher Parrock. In the earlier part of the twentieth century Laund became a Co-operative farm.

Carr Hall
From an 18th century engraving

Although this engraving of Carr Hall is somewhat stylised it is nevertheless reasonably accurate. If the chap sitting on a log (bottom right of picture) were to do this today he would be flattened by traffic when the Carr Road – Every Street traffic lights changed!

Frequent reference has been made to 'estates' within this text where the word is used in context to the land holdings of particular farms. However, to use the word in its true sense it is fair to say that only two landed properties within the history of Barrowford ever fitted the 'estate' description and they are Carr Hall and Park Hill. The Hall was built around 1580 and the Towneley family who occupied the property in its early years were the closest thing that the area had to true gentry - their influence upon the growth of the whole district cannot be overestimated.

In 1754 the Clayton line began at Carr with John Clayton J.P, of Little Harwood, who married Margaret, heiress of Richard Towneley of Carr Hall. The Claytons owned the whole of the Carr Hall estate and a great deal of land around Colne and Laneshawbridge including the Towneley Barnside estate. Thomas, the surviving son, became sheriff of Lancashire in 1808 and also reached the rank of Colonel of the Lancashire Militia.

At the age of 24 Elizabeth, the only daughter and heiress of Thomas Clayton, married Edward Every, second son of Sir Henry Every, of Eggington Hall in Derbyshire, on February 10th 1835. Thomas Clayton died two days after his daughter's marriage but he would be no doubt have been happy in the knowledge that the Clayton line would continue at Carr Hall. Edward Every, after obtaining royal permission to take the name and arms of Clayton, became the first of the Every-Claytons. Thomas was the last male representative of the Claytons of Little Harwood, where they had been resident in unbroken succession for more than 400 years. Until the death of his mother in 1780, he lived at Barnside, his sister Martha acting as housekeeper for him there and later for many years at Carr Hall.

Carr Hall

At the time of his marriage Colonel Edward Every-Clayton was an officer in the First Lancashire Militia and was stationed at the Burnley Barracks when he first met his future wife. In later years he was appointed County Magistrate and Deputy Lieutenant of the County. He came to live at Carr Hall in 1780 and was a talented artist - some of his sketches of Barrowford still survive.

Edward and Elizabeth had nine children, including twins Fanny and Edward. Following Elizabeth's death Edward married Eliza Halstead, of Hood House and heiress of Rowley, by whom he had four children. The youngest daughter, Amelia Jane Eliza, married Major T H Bairnsfather and became mother of Captain Bruce Bairnsfather, the noted cartoonist of World War I.

For several years after the death of his first wife, Colonel Every-Clayton remained at Carr Hall, but removed to Rowley Hall when his son Thomas Edward reached the age of 21. His remains are interred in the Halstead vault at St. Peter's Church, Burnley.

Carr Hall Lodge c.1910

Of the four children Edward Every-Clayton had by his second wife his eldest, Penelope, appears to have been somewhat headstrong. She threw a bundle of her clothes from the upstairs window of the Hall and left a note addressed to one of her sisters saying she had gone to London and that they should hear from her in the course of a few days. It was discovered she had taken a train to Manchester but no further trace could be found. Colonel Every-Clayton contacted a friend in London and a few days later received the information that he had found the fugitive and that she had been married the day before to a Signor Sabbatini, an officer in the Italian Legion stationed at the barracks at Burnley where the two had formed an intimate relationship. Penelope was described at the time as being; *'21 years of age and of interesting appearance.'* Her new husband was aged 25 and of a noble Italian family - Penelope later became an Italian Countess.

Thomas Edward Every-Clayton, who inherited Carr Hall from his mother, was of a retiring disposition and refused to associate himself with public affairs. He busied himself with the business of his estate and in his desire for privacy attempted to close down Carr Hall Road, which had been a toll road, in the 1860s. This caused conflict with the public over the right of way but eventually, after a great deal of legal wrangling, he relented and rented out the right of way over the road to the Nelson Local Board. On his death, in 1886, his eldest son, Henry Herbert, came into possession of Carr Hall but unfortunately he died in 1887, only a few days after his 21st birthday. Carr Hall then passed to his younger brother, Edward, and the long Towneley-Clayton-Every connection at Carr Hall came to an end. In 1892 the Nelson Leader carried the story that;

> *With regret Carr Hall, the home for many years past of the Every-Claytons, is about to be vacated by its present tenant and Mr Hezekiah Fletcher will become the new tenant of the Hall. The family of Every-Clayton is beloved and respected in Nelson and far beyond, not only for its memories and associations, but for the goodness of its present younger members.*

Familiar names then become associated with the Hall when it was sold to William Tunstill, of Reedyford House. In 1911 William's son, Henry, took over the Carr estate and eventually sold it to Wilkinson Hartley who made a number of alterations to the structure of the building. The estate was broken up at this time and parcels were sold to a number of developers who then built the terraced rows, and larger detached houses within the area. Wilkinson Hartley's widow remained at the Hall until her death in 1927.

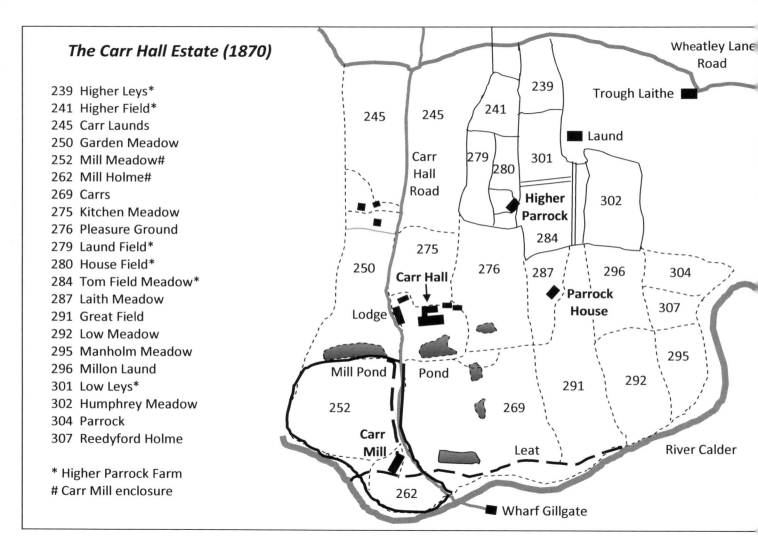

The Carr Hall Estate (1870)

239 Higher Leys*
241 Higher Field*
245 Carr Launds
250 Garden Meadow
252 Mill Meadow#
262 Mill Holme#
269 Carrs
275 Kitchen Meadow
276 Pleasure Ground
279 Laund Field*
280 House Field*
284 Tom Field Meadow*
287 Laith Meadow
291 Great Field
292 Low Meadow
295 Manholm Meadow
296 Millon Laund
301 Low Leys*
302 Humphrey Meadow
304 Parrock
307 Reedyford Holme

* Higher Parrock Farm
# Carr Mill enclosure

The Lime Trees, Carr Hall   *The above photograph was taken around 1918*

The lime trees ran along both sides of Carr Hall Road from its junction with Wheatley Lane almost down to Carr Hall Lodge. Planted in 1815 by Colonel Thomas Clayton the trees are probably the most popular subject to be found in old postcards of the Barrowford area. The saplings were presented to Colonel Clayton by local manufacturer, Richard Ecroyd, and were apparently planted out in the position of forward troops, with advance officers, to represent the Battle of Waterloo. Even though the erection of the detached houses along the eastern side of Carr Hall Road saw the removal of many of the 'soldier' trees some still remain within the gardens of these properties.

The lane here connects with the ancient inter-ridgeway track of Sandy Hall Lane and would have been a right of way for a very long time. Once the Carr Hall estate had settled its difference with the public over rights of passage along the lane it became an extremely popular route for walkers wishing to escape the mill towns in favour of the fresh air of Pendleside on holidays and weekends. For many years a building stood at the junction of Carr Hall Road and Wheatley Lane Road.

Living at Carr Hall in 1841 were Edward Clayton (40) independent, his wife Elizabeth (30) and children Penelope (5), Elizabeth (4), Caroline (2) and Thomas (2 months). Servants at the Hall were Sarah Walton (51), Mary Chadderton (50), Mary Dodd (15), Hannah Woodhead (15), Ellen Anderton (25), George Cutler (60), John Woodhead (15), Henry Heap (15) and Elizabeth Lawson (30).

Occupying Carr Mill were Ann Wheelhouse (65) a farmer and her son, William Wheelhouse (45), a corn miller. William's wife was Elizabeth (40) and their children were George (20), Sarah (20) and Samuel (15). The agricultural labourer at the mill was James Howarth (15). Living at the Lodge were James' grandparents John Howarth (60), a cotton weaver, his wife Mary (60) and Thomas Fell (40) an agricultural labourer along with his wife Maria (40) and son George (13).

Victoria Park c.1908

In 1892 the Nelson Local Board was formed and they absorbed 6 acres of former Barrowford land to the south of the Calder. This became Victoria Park: the photograph is taken looking towards the Carr Mill site

In 1861 Edward Every-Clayton, a Lieutenant in the Lancashire Militia, was the head of household at the Hall along with his wife Elizabeth (42) and children Elizabeth (24), Fanny (18), Edith (16), Annette (14), Harriet Ann (5), Edward Charles (3); Ellen (2) and Amelia Jane (6 months). Mary

Matida (34) came from Wellington in Summerset to be the children's governess while Alice White (37) a widow, had travelled from Scotland to work as the children's teacher. William Smith (19), from Eggington in Derbyshire, was the coachman, Sarah Settle (32), from Winslow in Cheshire, was the cook, Ann Boarman (26), from Chipping Norton in Oxfordshire, was the children's nurse, Ann Lawson (22) and her sister Elizabeth Lawson (23) were house maids. Elizabeth Ann Chaffer (18), from Northamptonshire, was a kitchen maid while her sister, Elizabeth Chaffer (26) was a parlour maid and Sarah Hargreaves (16), the only servant to have been born locally, was the children's under-nurse.

At the mill we find William Moon (41), a corn dealer, originally from Beamsley in Yorkshire, with his wife Isabella (31 -née Lister) from Thornton in Yorkshire while their children Mary Ann (3), Joseph (2) and William (2 months) were born in Barrowford. Isabella's brother, David Lister (34), is the corn miller and John Atkinson (18), from Bentham, is the mill carter. Two families are living at the Lodge where David Sutcliffe (53) is a labourer and head of family with his wife Amelia (51) and children Elizabeth (21), a cotton power loom weaver and Mary (14), also a weaver. Next door at the Lodge are Jonas Brown (23), a carter from Earby, his wife Jane (31) from Colne and young children Isabella (4), Margaret (2) and Lucy (2 months), all born in Barrowford.

The 1871 census shows that Thomas Edward Every-Clayton (30), a 'gentleman landowner,' is now head at Carr Hall, his wife Eliza Henrietta (31) was born in Bacup while son Henry Herbert (4) was born at Carr. Son Edward (3) was born at Watermillock in Cumbria while Ernest Leopold (2) was born at Carr as was the youngest child, George Frederick (2 months). Alice Murgatroyd (29) of Nelson was the cook and Emily Symonds (30) from Hertfordshire was a waitress. Elizabeth Wilcock (22) from Yorkshire was the nurse, Elizabeth Jancey (47) from Hampton in Northamptonshire was also a nurse while Martha Dyson (49) from Derbyshire was described as a 'monthly nurse.'

At the mill we see that Elizabeth Moon (36) is now head of household and a corn miller living with her brother John (33), also a corn miller, and servant Jane Phillips (57) of Halton in East Yorkshire.

David Sutcliffe (63), a labourer, is the widowed head at the Lodge living with his granddaughter Amelia Shoesmith (8), daughter Mary Grimshaw (24), a housewife, and son-in-law John Grimshaw (26), a stone mason. At Carr Hall Garden is James M Wight (44), a gardener from Dumfries and his oddly named wife Ellen Edward (47) from Stonehaven. Children are William M Wight (15), a twister from Dumfries, Anis J (11) born Tynnson? Elizabeth (9) born Cumberland, Jamie (5) born Reedley Hallows and Catherine (2) born in Barrowford. Also resident was Elizabeth Smart (4) a boarder from Wigton in Cumberland.

CARR RD. NELSON.

At Carr Hall Cottage John Watson (78), a 'size boiler' (taper), is head with Mary Ann his wife whose age is given as 31.

Carr Road Top, Nelson c.1906

The following census returns (1881) show Thomas Edward Every-Clayton (40) still in residence at the Hall with his wife Eliza (41) and children Constance (17), Florence (16), Herbert (14), Edward (13), Ernest (12), George (10), Maud (8) and Arthur (7). Servants are Emma Cain (17), a house maid from Oswestry in Shropshire, Jullienne Ockier (22), a servant from France, the delightfully named Pinkney Wormwell (23), the butler from Lothersdale, Margareta Voneschen (20) a housemaid from Rein in Switzerland and Emily Roberts (33) the cook from Shrewsbury in Shropshire.

At the mill we find Elijah Moon (45) who was a 'corn miller with four labourers,' Jane Phillip (66), a servant, and Joseph Proctor (19) a carter from Thornton in Yorkshire.

In 1881 we see that a Chestnut House has appeared on the Carr Hall estate and head of this household was Fergus Wilkinson (40) a cotton manufacturer from Roughlee and his wife Sarah (40) from Barrowford. The Carr Hall Garden House is occupied by James Lawson (38), a market gardener from Burnley, his wife Susan (36), from Roughlee and children Arthur (11), Thomas (8), Richard (6), Ellen (3) and Jane (1). The Singleton family live in the house where the top of Carr Hall Road meets with Wheatley Lane Road; here Joseph Singleton (38) from Thornton is an 'oatmeal bread baker' as is his wife Christina (45) from Burnley. The couple have one child named Montague (14) who is described as a scholar.

The census returns for the Carr Hall estate illustrate the wide demographic area from which the estate servants came. This, of course, was very common within the Victorian period when the industrial revolution had transformed whole districts from their former agrarian economy into factory-based production economies. The daughters of families, who would once have helped out on the family farm, or a neighbouring farm, were now faced with the stark reality of working for a pittance in a noisy, dirty factory or seeking work with any estate or well-to-do household that could provide them with suitable work. And so we see a demographically eclectic mix of backgrounds within the staff at Carr Hall during the nineteenth century.

Following WWII Carr Hall fell rapidly into a state of neglect and unfortunately the criteria of town and city Corporations at that time were based almost exclusively upon economy. *"Dry rot"* - that catch-all for Councils who do not have the gumption to preserve the finite history on their own doorstep – was wheeled out as the customary excuse and Carr Hall, for all its cultural and architectural importance, went the way of so many fine old buildings around the district when it was demolished in 1954. To this day the ghostly echoes of the Towneley and Every-Clayton families can be heard when stonework from the Hall is spotted incorporated into some river wall, or has been used to shore up an embankment here or there. Until relatively recently an amount of large carved stones from the hall were dumped by the river at Barrowford, where Pendle Water meets with Colne Water. The high river wall at Barrowford caul also contains a number of stone blocks that once witnessed the history of one of the finest halls within the entire district.

Carr Corn Mill

Until the Carr Mill was erected (around 1543) on the Towneley land of New Carr the people of Pendle Forest were required to grind their corn at the Bradley Mill in Marsden. In the later fifteenth century this situation was becoming untenable as the population increased and with it a higher demand for corn. Many of the Pendle farmers were in favour of a mill in the Roughlee district but the site at Carr was decided upon. The Towneleys ran the mill for which they paid an annual rent to the Clitheroe overlords.

The corn milling operations were often owned by members of the minor gentry or a coalition of local business men who would hold shares in the venture. The rights of these mill owners were jealously guarded and many disputes arose through farmers taking their corn to be ground at rival mills. In January 1657 Christopher Towneley, of Carr Hall and Mill, found himself indicted on a charge of wilful damage for which he was summoned to appear at the Pendle halmote court from where the case was referred to the Preston Assizes in April of that year. The Attorney General conducted the case in front of a jury picked from the Blackburnshire forest areas and the charges were stated to have been;

That Christopher Towneley of Carr in the county of Lancaster gent, John Varley of Carr aforesaid in the said county husbandman and George Pollard of Reedley Hallows in the said county carpenter did on the eighteenth day of December in the year of our Lord God one thousand six hundred and fifty six at Barrowford in the county of Lancaster by force and arms that is to say with staffs clubs and axes and other weapons of offence and did use them to mob riotously and did congregate and unlawfully assemble together to the great terror of the people of this Commonwealth with the intent to destroy by force and wantonly one mill caul standing upon a river called Barrowford which was set to supply a certain mill there called Barrowford Mill being in the possession of Christopher T[...] and James Wilson and did break and pull up by reason whereof the aforesaid mill was made useless to the great damage of them the said Christopher T[...] and James Wilson contrary to the laws of disorder in which this case is presented and contrary to the public peace.

Here we find that Towneley, in the true spirit of business enterprise, had attempted to knobble the rival corn mill at Barrowford (the 'mill in the park') by taking a couple of his estate workers along to destroy the mill caul. However, if the Barrowford Mill owners thought that they were to see justice done they were in for a disappointment; the judgment of the court was that there was insufficient evidence and so Towneley and his group of henchmen walked free.

The Barrowford Mill Caul prior to the floods of 1967 when the waterfall was subsequently lowered to half of its previous height

Carr Mill Caul
From a painting by Joseph Ogden

The caul at Carr Mill was situated roughly where the NE corner of the wall surrounding Nelson Cricket Field now stands. The painting (left) looks eastward along the River Calder towards Barrowford where the tower of St. Thomas' church can be made out. The caul, or weir, raised the water level in the river thus enabling it to be drawn off above the caul and directed via a water leat down to the mill pond or lodge (see the Carr Hall estate plan opposite).

Before Carr Road, leading down from Nelson, was upgraded in the later nineteenth century the access into the Carr Hall estate was via the lane of what is now Carr Hall Road. This trackway forded the Calder at the point where the modern Carr Road Bridge bisects Victoria Park and takes the road over the river. When the Calder was in spate people travelling into Marsden from the Carr Hall side of the river would have to walk along the west bank to Barrowford and then over the Reedy Ford. Jesse Blakey relates that a man named Abraham Uttley, a carter at Carr Mill, used to rent out a pair of tin boots to those not wishing to get their feet wet when crossing the Carr Ford. At one-halfpenny per return journey the boots would no doubt have paid for their initial cost many times over during the course of a number of years. Blakey also said that an athletic lady from the Hall was in the habit of pole-vaulting over the river.

On the Marsden side of the river stood a cottage with the name of Wharf Gillgate, Gillgate meaning *river ford*. It appears from the estate plan below that a small wharf existed here, connecting the river with the footpath. It is possible that was the site of a small ferry boat operation at some time, placed here to aid wheeled traffic taking corn to the mill when the river was too high to ford.

The Carr Mill Site (1847)

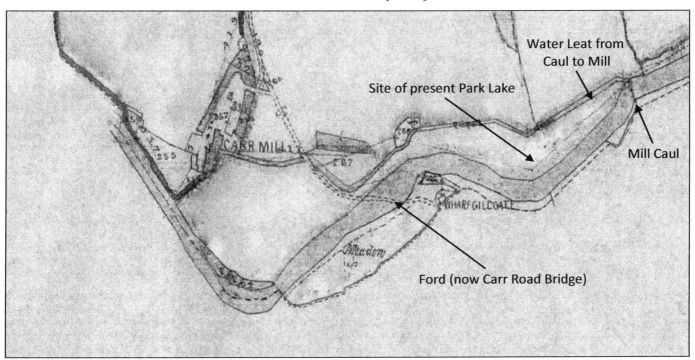

Carr Road Bridge

Site of the original ford and Wharf Gillgate Cottage

Having forded the Calder from the Carr Hall estate to the Marsden side of Carr Road bottom a footpath followed the river bank eastward to the river caul. A little further along the river the path, or trackway, entered a meadow sitting in the bend of the river across from Lower Clough Mill known as *The Holme Over The Water*.

This was formerly two acres of land attached to the Carr Hall estate and adjoining the land of the Reedyford Farm estate known as Reedyford Bridge Holme. The photograph earlier in this section shows haymaking in progress on the Bridge Holme and this meadow directly adjoins the Carr land of Holme Over The Water - this, in effect, brings us full circle to where we started this journey around the history of Lower Barrowford.

Central Barrowford

St. Thomas' Church

Introduction

Whereas **Lower Barrowford** covered the area of the township below a line drawn roughly north-south, and to the west of Holmefield House, the **Central Barrowford** section takes as its subject that area encompassed within the two boundaries of Holmefield House and Pasture Lane. Although the early township of Barrowford was split between *Blakey (Blacko)*, *Over Barrowford* and *Lower Barrowford* the later political boundaries created *Central Barrowford* and this is the general area of interest here.

The foundation of the 'village' of Barrowford (more properly an extended township) is akin to the beginnings of most other semi-rural villages and small towns in the East Lancashire district in that the farmers and smallholders of the early and late Medieval periods were the first to settle and farm the valley bottoms. Some of the rough peaty lands of the higher grounds, sloping upwards from the river valley on either side of Barrowford, were initially taken into cultivation by new settlers from the southern Saxon areas of England and from the Scandinavian districts. As the better valley lands were claimed newcomers had to cast their nets wider and they settled along the ridgeways and hillsides. Here, then, we find local farmsteads such as Higher Fulshaw which could well have been founded within the period before the coming of the Normans in 1066.

Eventually the newly cultivated lands were able to hold increasing numbers of sheep and the local trade in woollen goods expanded rapidly. The new breed of woollen merchants built their own smallholdings, such as Lower Fulshaw, in the 16th and 17th centuries and such was their prosperity that some of them moved into the valley to build their new mills where the river would supply the necessary mechanical power. Barrowford Old Mill might well have been the first of these enterprises but others quickly followed – in consequence we see the arrival of buildings that reflect the new wealth and status of the woollen manufacturers. Here we find the recorded history of Central Barrowford in sites such as Bank Hall and the White Bear along with the fascinating stories of the farmers and mill owners.

Central Barrowford in 1893 showing the area around the Fleece Inn at the bottom of Church Street

The Berry Family

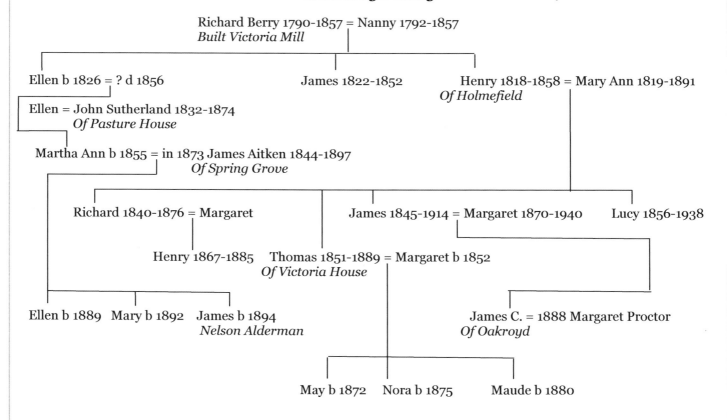

Richard Berry 1790-1857 = Nanny 1792-1857
Built Victoria Mill

Ellen b 1826 = ? d 1856   James 1822-1852   Henry 1818-1858 = Mary Ann 1819-1891
                                                          Of Holmefield

Ellen = John Sutherland 1832-1874
Of Pasture House

Martha Ann b 1855 = in 1873 James Aitken 1844-1897
Of Spring Grove

Richard 1840-1876 = Margaret   James 1845-1914 = Margaret 1870-1940   Lucy 1856-1938

Henry 1867-1885   Thomas 1851-1889 = Margaret b 1852
                    Of Victoria House

Ellen b 1889   Mary b 1892   James b 1894   James C. = 1888 Margaret Proctor
                             Nelson Alderman   *Of Oakroyd*

May b 1872   Nora b 1875   Maude b 1880

Berry's Victoria Mill

Richard Berry was one of the pioneers of the factory system within Barrowford. He was born in the final decade of the eighteenth century when handloom weaving was at its peak; however, when Richard had reached his twenties this was no longer the case. Spinning mills were springing up along the local rivers and canals and the consequent increase in available yarn meant that the days of the old handloom weaving process were numbered. Recognising this, the young Richard Berry set up a small cotton spinning operation sometime around 1815 in a building that stood in the vicinity of what is now the White Bear car park. Here the water from a mill lodge powered spinning frames and the yarn produced here was woven into cloth pieces.

Around this time Richard married Nanny and the couple lived in Jonathan Street where, in 1818, their first child, Henry, was born. In 1822 a second son, James, came on the scene and in the following year Richard and Nanny moved into one of a row of cottages they had built on lower David Street - here their only daughter, Ellen, was born in 1826. The Berrys provided room and looms for their weavers who would still be operating handlooms but on a more efficient level of production than the old home-based method. A building on Jonathan Street, adjacent to the Berry's first home, was used for clothlooking the finished pieces and this was possibly also where the weavers were housed. Gradually the output of their spinning and weaving operations increased and the Berrys built more houses around the Halstead Lane area for their workers. Eventually, in the late 1830s, Richard decided that the time was ripe for expansion and he built the riverside Victoria Spinning Mill on land called The Pastures.

Berry's Mill Weir

This wintry scene shows the frozen weir that supplied water to the mill boiler and engine. The buildings in the centre are the Old Row and Holgate Street shortly before demolition in the early 1960s. The area between the Old Row properties and the mill was known as Berry's Gap. When the mill was built (c.1840) the river was much wider here but was filled in so as to accommodate the mill and houses.

By 1841 Richard and Nanny had moved to Sutcliffe Row, which stood on the main road on the Higherford side of Halstead Lane, and in 1845 the firm of Richard Berry and Son was registered when Richard formed a partnership with his 27 year-old son, Henry Berry. Henry married Mary Ann and they had three sons, Richard, James and Thomas and a daughter, Lucy. Richard and Nanny Berry died in the same year of 1857 and in the following year their son, Henry, also died at the age of 40. This left Henry's wife, Mary Ann, to run the family estate assisted by her young sons Richard and James.

In 1861 Mary Ann and her children were living at Berry's House (later to be number 73 Gisburn Road) where she was the widowed head of household and a cotton manufacturer. Sometime within the following ten years Mary Ann built the imposing Holmefield House as, by 1871, she was living here with son James, a cotton spinner and manufacturer, son Thomas who was also a manufacturer, daughter Ellen Ann and Jane Percivell (20), a maid servant from Yorkshire.

Holmefield House

At Holmefield House, in 1881, the census returns show Mary Ann to have been a manufacturer and farmer of 1,319 acres and employing 279 full-time workers alongside 40 part-timers. Son James was also given the same status while daughter Lucy had no occupation. Also with the family were Mary Ann's grandson, Harry (13), and the maid servant, Amelia Alderson (22) from Airton in Yorkshire. By 1896 it appears that the only member of the family to be still living at Holmefield was Lucy Berry.

Thomas Berry

Thomas, the grandson of Richard and Nanny Berry, was educated at Huddersfield College and when he returned to Barrowford in 1869 he joined the family firm. Thomas, besides being an able businessman, was somewhat of a social reformer and as such he was instrumental in the provision of free education for the village. He was one of the initial School Board members in 1874 and was elected Chairman in 1886. He also occupied other important offices including Treasurer of the Gas Committee in 1886 and Overseer of the Poor for the Barrowford township in 1879 before being elected as Guardian of the township. Thomas was a dedicated Primitive Methodist within which circuit he became a local preacher, class leader and Sunday School teacher - he was sadly missed throughout the village when he died at the age of 38 in 1889.

Thomas married Margaret sometime after April 1871 and he moved his new wife into the family home at Berry's House, his mother having moved into her new home at Holmefield House. Although the census enumerators were fond of calling the house *'Berry's House'* the property was actually one of two dwellings built in 1837 by John Steel (1802-1856), a Barrowford tailor. Berry's House was called Victoria House and Springfield House stood adjacent. When Steel originally built Springfield House it became known as *'Cabbage Hall'* as a local rumour had it that he 'cabbaged' cloth from his customers (charging for cloth that was never used) but it is probable that local people were jealous of Steel's success as he also owned a large house in Newbridge and built the cottages there known as Clock Cottages in 1837.

Victoria House (73 Gisburn Road)

The house is under demolition here following compulsory purchase of the site by the County Council in the early 1970s. Also destroyed were the adjoining cottages of Foulds Street and Rushton Street (also known as the Club Houses). Victoria House had an old stone built workshop with an external staircase to the rear and the stonework from this can still be seen in the wall of the primary School.

A MUGA area for the use of the Rushton Street Primary School now occupies the site of Victoria House and Foulds Street

In 1881 Thomas and Margaret Berry were still living at Victoria House and they now had three daughters, May (b. 1872), Nora (b. 1875) and Maude (b. 1880). Also at the house was Ellen Morris (18) a servant from Madley in Shropshire. Neighbours of the Berry family, at Springfield House ('Cabbage Hall'), were William Tattersall, a tailor and draper, his wife Ellen, daughter Elizabeth and son, Starkie, also a tailor. In the neighbouring Rose Cottage were John Fieldhouse (58), a School Board clerk from Keighley, his wife Dorothy (46) born in Grassington and their children John (19), a joiner, Albert Sugden (15), a booking clerk at Nelson railway station, Sarah (10), a school monitor/mistress at the Board School, Elizabeth (9), Lucy Allen (7), Arthur James (4) and Annie Maude (5 months). Ten years previously the occupiers of Rose Cottage had been James C Morris (32), a doctor and surgeon from Wales along with his wife Emily (29), from Ireland and her sister, Frances Garde (22), with no occupation, from Cork – the brother of these ladies was Thomas H Garde, a watchmaker who was living at Crowtrees in 1891.

Victoria House and Mills: c.1900

75 Gisburn Road (shop)

Springfield House

Victoria (Berry's) House

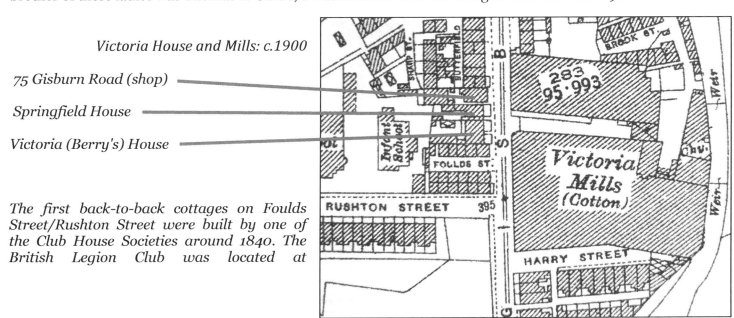

The first back-to-back cottages on Foulds Street/Rushton Street were built by one of the Club House Societies around 1840. The British Legion Club was located at

Springfield House in the middle part of the 20th century.

Thomas Berry's three children, May, Nora and Maude all gave their names to streets in Barrowford which were either built or were partly funded by the Berry's. Lucy Street, behind Holmefield House, was named after Thomas' Aunt Lucy of Holmefield while Harry Street was named after Thomas' nephew. Both Harry Street and Victoria Street were built by Henry Atkinson to house workers at Berry's Mill on land purchased from Mary Ann Berry of Holmefield. Following completion of building works the name of Victoria Street was transferred from the street at the rear of the row at 75 Gisburn Road and this was given the name of Butterfield Street. The houses on Victoria Street were built in 1875-76, Henry Atkinson paying rent for the land at £8: 10s: 4d until the houses were sold and he was able to pay Mrs. Berry in full. On 12th November 1876 John Clark, landlord and brewer of the Bridge Inn, agreed to purchase number 8 from Atkinson at a price of £155. Some of the other cottages were rented at £1: 5s: 9d per annum with a ground rent payable to the Lords of Pendle Forest of ½d per annum.

Victoria Street: 1925 (numbers 6 & 8 - backs)

At this time it was common practice for the landlords of public houses to put their spare money into property, as we have seen with John Clark. Following in his footsteps John Gabbatt purchased number 2 Victoria Street in 1877. Gabbatt was the son of a beer shop proprietor in the buildings on the main road across from the Gaumless Trough – unfortunately, along with many other small beer shop owners, Gabbatt's establishment was closed down following an Act of Parliament in 1867. John Gabbatt was a representatives of the Working Men's Institute - in 1898 John Strickland bought Bank Hall from Edwin H Cragg and went on to sell it to John Gabbattt and others for the sum of £587:10s. The property was then turned into the Lamb Working Men's Club.

The Berry's Victoria Mills had been expanding over the period from 1866 when it had been converted from a spinning mill to a weaving mill. In 1883 Thomas Berry extended the mill by demolishing the original spinning mill and extending sheds Number 1 and Number 2 to the main road. At this time a new Bracewell and Pickup steam engine was installed to power the 1,700 looms. Like their competitors throughout the district the Berry's were not immune from the vagaries of the cotton industry and there were occasions following the expansion of 1883 when they had need to lay off their workers or cut wages.

In 1890 there was a prolonged strike by the coal miners and by the end of March the mills of Barrowford were feeling the effects. Martha Ann Berry (cousin to Thomas) had married James Aitken who operated a successful coal retailing business from his canal wharf at Barrowford locks. James and Martha Ann lived at Spring Grove, next to Higher Park Hill Farm, from where James also ran his business as a supplier of town gas to the Borough of Nelson. The fact that his wife's cousin Thomas had been a big-wig on the Barrowford Gas Committee cannot have been a disadvantage to James Aitken but, nevertheless, when the coal began to run out at his storage warehouse he would have been unable to help keep the engines turning at Victoria Mills.

By the April of 1890 most of the mills and factories in Colne had been forced to close and James Berry, who had taken over Victoria Mills following the death of his brother Thomas, was forced to shut the mill down and lay off 600 workers for a week.

Victoria Mill Engine

When the mill started up again production was restricted to a four-day week of seven hours only. By May the coal stocks at Nelson railway station were down to a few tons and the shortage started to affect the public; where the price of one hundredweight of the black stuff had been 9d before the strike the cost had now doubled. Luckily many people had sufficient reserves in their coal-sheds to see them through the worst of the shortage.

Thomas Berry had died the year before the coal strike leaving his widow and children in residence at Victoria House in 1896. Thomas' mother, Mary Ann, died in 1891 and, as we have seen, Thomas' brother James ran the family business of cotton manufacturing, property owning and farming. James was, in fact, very keen on the farming side of the business and he enjoyed breeding heavy farm horses. It would appear that he was successful at this as he frequently won first prize for *'best mare for road or field'* at the Great and Little Marsden Agricultural Shows.

Berry's Victoria Mill: 2009

The extant building with the lift tower protruding from the roof is the warehouse built in 1866. Number One weaving shed occupied what is now the car park (the outline of the saw-tooth 'northern light' roof of the shed can be clearly seen on the side of the warehouse). To the left of the warehouse stood the Number Two shed extension erected in 1883. The square chimney rises above the oldest remaining part of the mill

In 1896 James Berry had left his sister Lucy in occupation of Holmefield House and, according to a trade directory, was living at Oak Mount on Gisburn Road. James died in 1914 and in the following year, possibly instigated by his son (James C Berry) R. Berry and Son became a limited company with a guarantee of £50,000 in £1 shares. In 1929 the firm became a part of Hindley Brothers Ltd. until its closure in 1955 when a part of the mill was taken over by Halsteads (shuttle makers) and Edwin T Riddiough and Company Ltd. (sheet metal workers and caravan accessory suppliers). The front of the Number One Shed became Jackson and Hanson's Victoria Garage and the Talbot Plating Company took over the old engine and boiler house site.

James C Berry inherited his father's enthusiasm for agriculture and he sponsored a silver cup for the poultry section of the Barrowford and District Horticulture and Allotment Society. The Society was based at 155 Gisburn Road (near to the Council Offices site) until the property was demolished around 1960 – the Society is still active today. James C Berry married Margaret Proctor in June 1888 and they lived at a house variously given in records as Oak Mount, Oak Bank and Oakroyd. Margaret was the daughter of Thomas and Eleanor Proctor who at one time kept the White Bear. Eleanor had also been the landlady of the Moorcock and the Bay Horse at Roughlee – she died aged 84 in 1910.

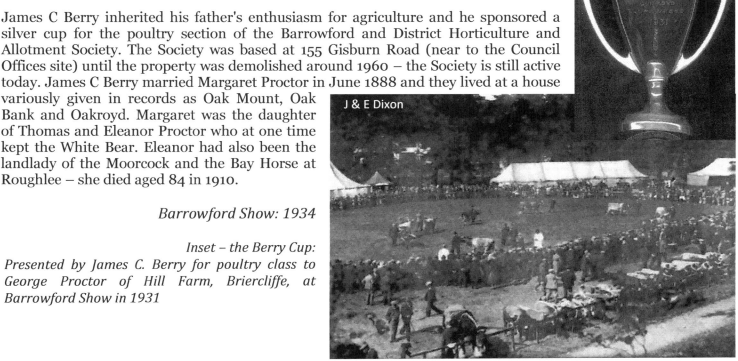

J & E Dixon

Barrowford Show: 1934

Inset – the Berry Cup:
Presented by James C. Berry for poultry class to George Proctor of Hill Farm, Briercliffe, at Barrowford Show in 1931

Workers at Berry's Mill

The photograph would have been taken not too long before the mill closed in 1955. The chap on the right with his 'loom key' would be a tackler. The double beam looms are set up for stripes and are weaving towelling

Back O' Berry's: 1960s
Original: Jim Sanderson

The high wall (right of picture) is the only remnant of Richard Berry's original spinning mill from around 1840. This was pulled down in 1883 to make room for the Number One weaving shed. A weir was situated here before it was superseded by the one higher upstream

Barrowford Police Station

The first purpose-built Police Station in the village was erected directly opposite to Holmefield House in 1896-7 and housed the sergeant and constable (pictured here with their wives shortly after the station was opened). The police pillar standing on the pavement housed a telephone to be used to contact the policemen when the station was closed.

The new Police Station was erected on land known as Berry's Little Field, once part of Berry's Farm. This latter stood on Portland Street and later became a garage run by Cuthbert Berry, one of the manufacturing family. The farm buildings were replaced by single storey buildings used as a garage until they were removed to accommodate housing in 2008. Large stepping stones forded the river behind the farm and allowed access from Corlass Street to the Bull Holme until the floods of 1967; the well that supplied the farm is now beneath the police Station.

It is not clear when the first permanent police presence was provided in Barrowford but two constables were stationed here by 1841:– PC James Brown, aged 30, boarded at the Fleece Inn while his colleague, Isaac Wood (30), lived with his Irish-born wife, Mary (40), on James Street. In 1848 PC Horan was one of the village constables and on 29th April of that year we see him involved in what would have been a typical police matter in the village. At the Burnley Petty Sessions Ellis Smith, of Barrowford, was charged with pilfering 16 gooseberry trees from Henry Howarth's garden. PC Nicholas Horan gave evidence that

Howarth saw his trees on the Saturday but they had gone by the following Sunday morning. Howarth informed PC Horan who went to the allotments and found the missing trees in Smith's garden *'all planted in a nice little row.'* Smith then went to Howarth's house and said he had never seen the trees before and that for the life of him he could not understand how they had appeared there! With great generosity of spirit Smith informed Howarth that he could have his trees back if he collected them. Howarth went to look at the trees and recognised them from their *'reeky'* (reddish) appearance – the trees had recently been purchased from a sale at a Burnley timber yard. The court ordered Smith to pay 2d each for the trees and a further 2s:8d for trespass.

By 1861 a cottage on the Alma Row (above the George and Dragon) was being used to house the village police constable where we find Robert Metcalfe (48) with his wife Alice (46) and their 6 children. Metcalfe (originally from Milnthorpe in Westmoreland) had been the constable in Barrowford since at least 1852. On June 2nd 1860 PC Metcalfe appeared at Colne Court as a prosecution witness against Henry Hartley of The Ing Farm in Barrowford. Hartley was charged by Mr Jesse Yewdall, the worsted inspector from Keighley, with being in possession of a large quantity of 'rouge,' or 'wasted,' and other goods consisting of Angola yarn etc. of which he could give no proper account. Following a tip-off the inspector, along with PCs Lowe and Metcalfe, found a number of bags of rouge concealed about Hartley's house. Some were hidden in the oven, some were stuffed in the bed and yet more had been jammed in behind the furniture. The prisoner could only account for 10-12 lb of the very large quantity of yarn and, being found guilty, was fined £20 – if he could not pay he was to be imprisoned for one month.

A Nelson Policeman c.1885

In 1868 John Holgate was a Barrowford constable at the Alma Cottages and by 1871 PC William Rigby Hill had been transferred here from Colne. Around 1877 the police constable was James Elliott (40), from Dumfries, who was living in one of the Club Houses in 1881 along with his wife Agnes (39) and 4 children. By the time of the next census in 1891 Thomas Wilson (50), from Burton-in-Lonsdale, was the village police sergeant and lived at 75 New Road (Gisburn Road) with his wife Elizabeth (50), from Lancaster, and their unmarried daughter Elizabeth (29). Also at 75 New Road were PC John Simpson (40), from Durham, who had been transferred from Foulridge in 1890, his wife Selina (35), also from Durham, and their 3 sons.

PC Joseph Ingleson lived at 62 Gisburn Road in 1896 and was the last policeman to live in private accommodation - within a matter of months the new station at 20-22 Gisburn Road opened and provided living quarters for two families. In 1933 John Hopper was the resident sergeant and his constable was Ronald Almond. By 1946 resident at the station were sergeant C Bamford and constable J L Minshaw. During the great flood of 1967 the Barrowford constable related how he opened the front door of the station just in time to rescue the kennel that had been in the station yard and was now floating down the road with the bewildered police dog still inside! Two years later Barrowford lost its resident police presence when the station closed - the building became the Holmefield Teaching Centre where the immigrant population were taught language skills. At the time of writing (2009) the building has been unoccupied for a number of years.

Tram outside Portland House: c.1930

Bolton's Grocery and Decorators
Miss Clara Bolton outside
70 Gisburn Road c.1920

Across from the Police Station, on the Higherford side of Portland Street, stands the end property of Portland House. This row of houses was built on to the southern end of Corlass Houses which were the first dwellings to be erected within this immediate area. William Corlass ran Hodge Bank Mill, at Reedyford, from 1806 to 1831 and built the earliest tranche of Corlass Houses as weaver's cottages in 1824. Before this the old road from Marsden to Gisburn ran alongside the river and the new Corlass Houses separated the old road from the new turnpike road, thus effectively closing off the original road forever. The Corlass row were back-to-back houses; the backs fronted onto Corlass Street which can still be seen as the only remaining length of the ancient highway.

At the far end of Corlass Street stands the row of 2-6 Victoria Street where, on the end of this street, we find Stanley Place (64-66 Gisburn Road) and the two shops at 68-70 Gisburn Road. As was the case with the houses of Victoria Street these properties were built by Henry Atkinson on land belonging to Mary Ann Berry of Holmefield House. In 1877 Doctor John Lord purchased the two properties of Stanley Place from Atkinson for the sum of £600 on a lease of 999 years. Dr Lord moved his wife, Jean, and 7 year-old daughter, Margaret Ellen (Nellie), and 5 year-old Jane Elizabeth into Stanley Place in the April of 1877 and the family (with the addition of son John in 1878) lived there until 1896 when the property was sold to John Bolton, a painter and decorator who occupied the neighbouring shop at number 68. John Bolton paid Dr Lord £680 for the property, £400 of which he borrowed from the Burnley Building Society. The Boltons were a well established Barrowford family, the head of which had been John Bolton of the Hubby, a cottage that stood across from the old St. Thomas' church until 1870. John Bolton, of Stanley Place, had 4 children; Alice, Clara, Clement and Vina – Clement followed in his father's footsteps as a decorator.

From the age of 10 or 11 Doctor Lord's daughter, Nellie, was a school mistress at the Board School (infants) which was housed in the Primitive Methodist Chapel on Church Street:

Front row L-R - Nellie Atkinson - Vera Stansfield – Priscilla Catlow – Janie Nelson

Middle row L-R – Sarah Proctor – Ruth Nutter – Lizzie Duckworth – Willie Robinson – Stanley Ashworth – Dinah Stow – Fred Firman

Back row L-R – Maggie Bannister – Janie Atkinson – S. Brown – Annie Nelson – Ivan Pate – **Miss Nellie Lord** - Maggie Atkinson – Willie Pickover – Willie Jackson

Barrowford Board School: 1882

Doctor John Lord

On 17th June 1917 John Bolton conveyed the property of Stanley Place to his children and in February 1922 Vina Bolton married William Hargreaves at the Congregational Chapel on Church Street. In April 1924 Alice Bolton married Frederick Rawson at the Congregational Chapel and in 1927 Clement Bolton died. In November 1932 the property of Stanley Place was rendered freehold when the Clitheroe Estate Company, who were the Lords of the Forest of Pendle, extinguished all manorial incidents saved by an Act of 1922 (Part V) – in other words, for a sum of £6: 3s: 1d all rents, fines and fees were discharged by the Estate Company.

In the 1880s and 90s the grocery shop at number 70 Gisburn Road was run by Timothy Duckworth, whose brother was a wholesale confectioner on Church Street. Sometime before 1918 Clara Bolton had taken over the grocery shop and her brother, Clement, was running the decorating business next door at number 68. By 1946 Clara had retired and was living with her widowed sister, Alice Rawson, at number 66 (Stanley Place) - living next door at 64 were their sister Vina and her husband, William Hargreaves. By this time number 68 had become a watchmaker and jewellers shop run by Frank Hall, living at the back was Harry Holt, a twister at Berry's Mill, and the grocery shop at number 70 was a hairdressers run by Mrs. A Chamberlain. Clara Bolton died in 1954, Alice Rawson in 1958 and Vina died in April 1960, her cousins inherited Stanley Place in 1961 and turned number 64 into two flats - 66 being sold at that time.

Jean Lord (left) with Nellie Lord and Perks the dog: c.1890

78–86 Gisburn Road

Continuing along this side of the road towards Higherford the two smaller cottages of 74 and 76 Gisburn Road, at the end of Harry Street, were contemporary with the nearby properties of Foulds Street and Victoria House (1837-40). It is likely that all these houses were built to house workers for the new Victoria Mills.

On the Higheford side of the mill a row of weavers cottages (pictured right) stood fronting onto the main road where the flats of Riverway and Fountains now stand. In 1891 John Emmott and his family lived at number 84 (photograph - second house from the left) where they had moved from their former home on Church Street. Throughout the latter quarter of the 1800s John Emmott ran a mineral water manufacturing business at number 2 Old Row (near to Berry's Mill). Emmott had been born in Burnley in 1842 and married a Barrowford girl named Mary Butterfield (b. 1844) who was the daughter of Thomas Butterfield of Pasture Gate Farm and later of Oaklands Home Farm on Church Street.

On the same day in 1872 John married Mary and her sister, Sophia Butterfield, married John's friend, Hartley Duckworth. Around the middle of the nineteenth century the extended Butterfield family were responsible for building property in the area and they gave their name to Butterfield Street some time after it had changed from Victoria Street in 1876. Hartley Duckworth was of the family who built Duckworth Street and owned a number of properties in the Church Street area.

John Emmott

By the year 1901 John Emmott had become an executive of the Barrowford Liberal Party and, at the time of his death, on 20th August 1905, he had become a Justice of the Peace, was president of the Ambulance Association and Chairman of the Sanitary and Buildings Committee (the equivalent of the modern Town Planning Committee). It appears that the mother of John Emmott's wife, Mary, was the daughter of Henry Holt, who owned land and property in Barrowford. Records show that Henry Holt left to Thomas Butterfield and his wife one-third of the properties of numbers 54 and 56 Gisburn Road and number 15 Corlass Street. In 1873 these properties, plus the ground of Corlass Street, were owned by Thomas Butterfield, cordwainer and Chelsea Pensioner, of Pasture Gate Farm, and Thomas Holt in trust for Mary Copley of Barrowford.

The First Barrowford Local Board 1892

Back row L-R – J.C. Waddington –James Dugdale – R. H. Wiseman – James Bracewell – Thomas Faraday

Second row L-R – John Hartley – Daniel Nutter – James Baldwin – Martin England – Dr. Pim

Front row L-R – John Emmott (resting his arm on his knee) – J. C. Howson – J. Whittingham

Embroidery Tester - Grace Emmott: 1886

In December 1874 John and Mary Emmott had a daughter, Grace, and her sister Margaret followed in 1880. Grace attended the Board School (infants) at the Primitive Methodist Chapel on Church Street and later moved to the senior school held in the neighbouring Congregational Chapel. In October 1886 Grace was a standard Year Five pupil and as such she was expected to show the skills she had learned by producing an embroidery tester (pictured right).

By 1901 the Emmott family had moved into one of the newly built houses of number 5 Forest View, on the main road to the front of Sam Holden's Holmefield Mills. John was still a mineral water manufacturer and both his daughters were weavers. On Friday 25th August 1905 the Nelson Leader announced that: '*It is with deep regret that today we announce the death of Councillor John Emmott of Barrowford. The sad event took place on Sunday morning, after a brief but painful illness, an internal complaint causing him great suffering, although for a time he was unconscious.*'

As for John's daughter, Grace Emmott, the plot takes a distinctly sad turn as the following report in the Nelson Leader of Friday September 2nd 1910 shows:

'*At the Barrowford Council Offices on Friday afternoon the East Lancashire Coroner held an inquest touching the death of Grace Emmott, a weaver of 5 Forest View, Barrowford, who was found drowned in a waterway leading from a lodge near Crow Trees House to Higherford Mill on Wednesday night.*'

'The first witness called was Mrs Mary Emmott, mother of the deceased. She said her daughter had not been very well lately, but continued to work until Wednesday. The deceased that day went to see a Doctor who gave her a bottle of medicine. On Wednesday night she seemed very cheerful and proceeded to visit some friends at Crow Trees House. That was the last time the witness saw her alive.'

'By Mr. Waddington: She had complained about her work at the mill, and it had preyed upon her mind.'

'Mr Procter: Did your daughter mention any name in her complaint? - Yes. Did she say she was treated unkindly? - No, not lately but there were little bits of things. Had she worked at Berry's Victoria Mills a long time? - Yes. Under the same overlooker? – Yes for a long time.'

'Witness further said that her daughter complained of very peculiar feelings coming over her.'

'Janet Atkinson, residing at Crow trees, said the deceased came to their house on Wednesday night. She was very quiet, and a little bit strange. Deceased also said to the witness 'Can you smell ammonia, Janet?' Witness replied, 'No; why?' and deceased said, 'Because I can smell it.'

'The deceased then walked with the witness towards the tram terminus a distance of 20 yards, and then returned to the house. The witness caught the eight o' clock tramcar.'

'P.C. Mulroy stated that at 9.30 on Wednesday night the last witness informed him that the deceased was missing. The Coroner: Did they say why they had told you? - Yes, they had found a bottle containing ammonia on the bank of the watercourse, and had become alarmed. The witness added that the stream ran past the end of the gardens at Crow Trees. The Coroner: I still don't understand why they should have come to tell you. Anyone might have left the bottle there. Witness: The fact that she had mentioned ammonia had aroused their suspicions.'

The Higherford Mill Race: Scene of Grace Emmott's Tragic Death

'The witness said that he found the body about 10.45 under a culvert. The water at the spot was between 4 and 5 feet deep. The deceased's mouth was slightly discoloured. He tried artificial respiration for an hour before the arrival of Dr. Burbridge, and it was continued for a further hour without success. The witness also stated that Mrs. Mary Emmott identified the bottle.'

"The Coroner, having intimated that this was all the evidence, Mr. Procter said he would like to call a witness (Grace's overlooker at the mill). *The Coroner: I don't think it is necessary. Something appears to have upset this woman. She evidently became low spirited, and when a person got into this condition there was no accounting exactly for them making use of somebody's name. His opinion was that she had taken a little of the ammonia, and then jumped into the water, being of unsound mind at the time. A verdict of 'Suicide whilst of unsound mind' was returned. The jury passed a vote of condolence with the family of the deceased.'*

The tragedy of Grace Emmott's death understandably had a profound effect on her mother, Mary - within two years the Nelson Leader of 9th August was carrying the following tribute:

'Another old Barrowfordian has just passed away in the person of Mrs. Emmott of Forest View. She had been unwell for two or three years and gradually grew worse until the end came on Saturday evening. She suffered greatly for several days prior to her demise but she bore her suffering patiently.

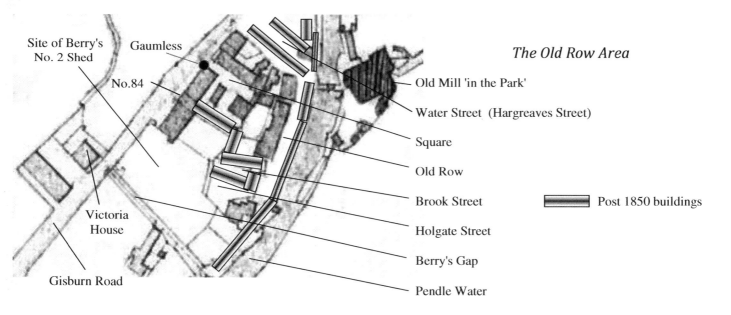

Site of Berry's No. 2 Shed
Gaumless
No.84
Victoria House
Gisburn Road

The Old Row Area

Old Mill 'in the Park'
Water Street (Hargreaves Street)
Square
Old Row
Brook Street
Holgate Street
Berry's Gap
Pendle Water

Post 1850 buildings

Behind John Emmott's house (at 84 Gisburn Road) stood a close-knit group of cottages and workshops collectively known as the Old Row. It is fair to say that this area formed the southern edge of central Barrowford, the core of early development stretching from here to Halstead Lane. The village 'centre' is actually somewhat of a misnomer in that Barrowford never was a village – technically it comprised a number of 'booths,' or farmsteads, within the post-Norman vaccary farming system.

As more land was taken into cultivation, especially from the fifteenth century, there was an incremental increase in farms and associated buildings and these were grouped into townships. We see, then, that Barrowford is properly an area made up of the townships of Blacko, Over Barrowford and Lower Barrowford. Lower Barrowford covered much of the district from Park Hill down to the Nelson boundary at Newbridge. As Barrowford developed this was found to be unsatisfactory in that the political boundaries were too far apart and so Barrowford Central was created – this, then, is roughly the area covered by this book.

Old Row from the Old Mill

The plan of the Old Row (previous page) shows the existing buildings of 1840 and the interposed properties that were built as the area rapidly expanded in response to the building of new mills. The first buildings here were erected as cottages to house the workers at the Old Mill (in the park), some of the houses being built by the mill owners. A bridge connected the Old Row with the Mill Holme on which the Old Mill stood - it had been removed by the time the above picture was taken but the site can still be made out within the river wall (seen here at the end of the street where the wall is recessed). One of the earlier buildings was the Dandy Shop which stood by the river at the end of Water Street (to the right of the bridge site). This three storey building was an early factory in as much as it was built to house a number of handlooms on the upper floors, the top floor being reached by means of an external stone staircase so that the weavers did not have to disturb the people on the lower floors.

Holgate Street: 1934

In addition to the Dandy Shop the row of properties on Water Street also housed shops and 11 cottages that were rented by the township from the Hartleys of Fulshaw Farm for the purpose of providing housing for the needy. Those who lived here were generally the poor and the elderly who, with no other means of support, were supplied with handlooms on which they could weave cloth pieces in exchange for their keep. At one time Old Laund Hall was also used as the Poor House for the more unfortunate people of Barrowford. In the late nineteenth century Water Street also housed the Liberal Club and Totty's slaughterhouse. This latter building was used for this purpose until the middle of the twentieth century when it was last occupied by local butcher, Philip Hanson senior, of Lower Fulshaw Farm.

The Old Row could almost be described as having been a hamlet within its own right and the people inhabiting the houses here were a close-knit community who worked their handlooms using yarn from the local spinning mills and then selling the finished cloth pieces back to the mill owners and cloth merchants. By the time that the later buildings in the Old Row appeared (the 1850s and 1860s) many of the former handloom weavers had taken work in the local mills as power loom weavers.

The Old Gaumless Fountain: pre-1911

The 'Old Gaumless' trough stood by the side of Gisburn Road at the entrance to The Square (its replacement can be seen in situ at the bottom of the picture below). In 1847 Oddie Sutcliffe, a yeoman of Bank Hall (the Lamb Club) and Henry Armistead, a cotton spinner, sank a bore hole at West Hill in order to supply their properties with fresh water. Such was the volume of water from the new source that they were able to pipe the surplus down the hill to the Old Row area. The clean water supply was welcomed by the local residents as they were able to obtain their domestic supply without having to walk to one or other of the spouts in the district. One of these spouts already existed near to Berry's Mill but the flow was somewhat sporadic - the Gaumless supply proved to be far more reliable.

The Square

However, the new Gaumless trough was far from ideal as horses drank from it, butchers sharpened their bloody knives on the gritstone edge and dogs were in the habit of topping up the water level! In 1911 an agreement was brokered between the Local Board and landowner John Holt whereby the corner of The Square, upon which the Gaumless stood, would be taken over by

the village. In 1913 John Holt donated the land and Councillor Christopher Atkinson, of Willow Bank (a cotton manufacturer at Lower Clough Mills) and his wife commissioned a brand new trough made out of polished granite and donated it to the village as a retrospective Coronation memorial fountain. The original Gaumless trough was sent into retirement on a Blacko farm. In 2005 local man Ian Wainman noticed that the old trough was being offered to sale and was about to leave the district that it had served for many years. Ian managed to persuade the local and Borough councils that the trough should be reinstated in its original home and so we see it today in all its old glory - standing aged but not bowed in close proximity to the later trough, not very far from its original position.

Barrowford at that time was able to boast a number of poets among its number who were only too keen to burst into print at the slightest of excuses. Many were the wordy efforts of the local populace in relation to the delights of the sylvan Pendle Water, the soaring dignity of the Old Roman Bridge or the fairy glens of Utherstone Woods. A local character by the name of Albert Veevers could always be relied upon for a few stanzas when the need arose and the old Gaumless did not escape his wit as the following extract from a 16 verse epithet shows:

For outward and for inward pains, 'Tis handy and most willing,
'Tis also good for window panes, When they are wanting swilling.

Albert was from a large family who owned properties on Church Street and, as a young man, he trained as a joiner. Unfortunately he fell from scaffolding at the age of 21 and landed on his head. Although he survived he was never able to work again and so he set himself up as an early form of marriage guidance counsellor:

Albert Veevers – Professional Peace Maker
9 Church Street, Barrowford
(Note the address - - Ancestral Residence - - A New Departure)

Whatever Brawls Disturb the Street
There should be peace at Home
When Wife and Husband are Unsweet
To Sweeten them I'll Come

Marriage in Trouble?
Albert Veevers – Park Hill
Phrenologist and Physiognomist
The Greater the Fee the Greater the Stimulus

In 1866 the Nelson Gas Company gained a licence to supply water to the public but they never brought a supply to Barrowford - in the same year the Nelson Local Board acquired the licence from the Gas Company and set about constructing the Walverden, Waids House and Coldwell reservoirs. On completion the Board were able to construct a 4 inch water main along the main road through Barrowford as far as the Fleece Inn at the bottom of Church Street, and a 3 inch pipe was carried along to the Higherford Weslyan Chapel. In 1871 the main pipe was extended from the Fleece Inn along Church Street to the Clough Springs brewery at the personal expense of the brewery owners, Messrs. Robert Hartley and Alexander Bell.

In 1886 the Government granted powers for the creation of large reservoirs at Ogden and Black Moss and for an auxiliary underground service reservoir and station at the top of Pasture Lane. However, it was not until 1912 that the Ogden reservoir water was filtered by a new plant at Barley and the service reservoir at Pasture Lane was not constructed (a site at Ridgealing finally being settled upon) until 1928.

Ogden Clough: 1905
The water from upper Ogden Clough was harnessed to create the Ogden Storage Reservoir at Barley

Until the Ridgealing station came on-stream in 1929 a number of Barrowford properties were still without mains water – Ford Street, for instance, was still supplied by water from the Bogmoriles Spring that was situated on the hill to the east of Mosley Street (which later became Queen Street).

PENDLE.
(OGDEN)

Besides the obvious benefits of not having to carry buckets of water around the streets the provision of clean running water to every household improved the health of the nation in no small way. Before the sewer system was developed in Barrowford (in the later 1800s) the outside 'long-drop' toilets attached to

each row, or block of dwellings, emptied either into a 'night-soil' pit or directly into the river. Moreover, other domestic and industrial detritus was thrown into the river and this, of course, was highly unhygienic. Where sewers existed new houses were often built with the addition of the new 'tippler' toilet system where waste water from the kitchen sink drained into a cistern and was then tipped into the toilet in order to flush it. The Burnley firm of Duckett and Son were at the forefront of this new technology and their tippler systems were fitted to new houses across the country. The firm were also leaders in the new 'flush' toilets and their *Duckett's Clencher* toilet bowl was highly thought of.

The Duckett Clencher and the toilet block that served the whole Square

Before the advent of clean water for all households the incidence of typhoid was widespread. In 1877 there was a major outbreak in Barrowford when at least 50 people were diagnosed with the disease and the authorities were at a loss to locate the source. Eventually the cause of the outbreak was traced to a farm in Blacko where the farmer, his wife and two daughters had been suffering from typhoid but had carried on milking their cows. The milk was then delivered around the village with the consequence that many of the farmer's unfortunate customers contracted the disease. The farmer had been totally unaware that he had been spreading the infection and was contrite when he learned the truth - in the end around eight people in the village died during the outbreak.

Mr and Mrs Richard Greenwood
75 Gisburn Road: c.1920

Across the road from the Old Row and Berry's Number Two Shed were, as we have seen, the higher status properties of Springfield House and Victoria House and, directly across from the trackway that originally led to Berry's old mill (Berry's Gap) stands the grocery shop of number 75 Gisburn Road. Mr and Mrs Greenwood are pictured here outside their shop around 1920 and in the 1950s the shop was owned by the Dixon family who also owned the back-to-back cottage to the rear that is number 3 Butterfield Street. The row of properties from the shop to Ingham Street were known as Victoria Buildings and along the back of the row a stream once flowed from its source near to Fulshaw Head, across Church Street and down Ingham Street. The stream then followed along Butterfield Street (beneath number 3) and along behind Victoria House. When the Board School was built, around 1896, the stream was directed through a tunnel along the length of the bottom school wall and still flows there today where it meets with another stream that runs from the corner of the old St. Thomas' churchyard and down to the bottom of Oaklands Avenue – the combined waterway then runs down the village and empties into the river to the south of the Clock Cottages.

Crossing Ingham Street, the long row of houses and shops fronting the main road show a varied history, most of them being of late nineteenth century construction. However, the block of three storey shops at the Higherford end of the row (101–103 Gisburn Road) are of interest. These properties were erected in

the early nineteenth century as back-to-back loom shops to house handloom weaving families, the rear dwellings being located on Hill Top. Around the middle of the nineteenth century the three roadside properties were converted into retail shops and the end one (number 103) served as a butchers shop for well over a century.

John Totty's Shop: 103 Gisburn Road
Courtesy of Philip Hanson

The Totty family with prize-winning cattle they would have recently purchased at the Great Marsden Show. The shop on the left (at 101a) was Whipp's grocery

From 1896 John Totty ran his butchery business from Number 103. He was possibly the son of John Totty, a butcher who came to Barrowford from Nelson in the 1870s and went bankrupt in 1877. John Totty ran his shop until J. S. Rushford took over in 1937 and he stayed here until 1949 when Green and

THIS IS OUR ORDINARY SHOW.

J. TOTTY. BUTCHER. BARROWFORD.   COME AND SEE OUR CHRISTMAS SHOW.

Hill Top Cottages

Son bought the business – Eddie Green ran the shop through to the 1960s. In the 1850s-60s the shops on the lower side of the three storey buildings were added and among the traders here were J. Townend and Sons, tailors – Fred Scarborough, a baker at 97c and A. Slater, general broker and furniture dealer at 97a. The Slaters were farmers from Roughlee and by the middle of the twentieth century John Slater and his brother were running a corn and seed business at 97a which replaced an earlier business of that type further down at 81 Gisburn Road.

Behind the row of 101-103 Gisburn Road stood a complex of houses that are now lost to us - in the eighteenth century some of these cottages were thatched. The family of Thomas Nowell lived in the largest house in this area and farmed the Lower Hubby Farm on Church Street. Most of these old houses were demolished to make way for the new Congregational Chapel in 1880 – this building was designed by the architect, John Gibson (1811-1887), who also designed the area known as 'New Town' in Scarborough. Before the Congregational Chapel had reached its 100th year it followed a great number of other important buildings into eternal obscurity. On the steep hill behind 103 Gisburn Road stood a row of five old cottages known as Hill Top. This quaint row housed a number of characters over its lifetime; one of these was Granny Birtwistle who, in the 1920s-30s, held séances in her cottage during which local people reported that the teapot would dance alarmingly around the table.

The Congregational Chapel:
Awaiting demolition in 1975

The new Congregational Chapel was very much a product of the imagination of the Barrowford 'Congo's' minister, the Reverend Edward Gough BA. Rev. Gough arrived in Barrowford in 1862 and very quickly built a strong following here. Within two years of his arrival he had married Sarah Corlass, the daughter of business man Thomas Corlass of Croft House. Rev. Gough originally lived at Beanfield House in Higherford before settling at 'The Minister's House' (Aubern House) on Halstead Lane. Born in Malton, Yorkshire, in 1836 the Reverend was a friend of John Gibson who was also from Malton, and it is little surprise that he asked his architect friend to design the new chapel. Rev. Gough's ministry in Barrowford lasted from his official inception in 1863 through to his retirement in 1915 - a period of 52 years. He died in Barrowford in 1917.

As was the case with other northern mill towns there was a prolific non-conformist movement within the burgeoning populace of Barrowford and not least among the new Methodist and Congregationalist groups were the leaders in society – a number of local business people were instrumental in the setting up of meeting houses in the early part of the nineteenth century where a licence would be obtained so that cottages could be used for religious meetings by the Independent, Primitive and Wesleyan Methodists, along with the Congregationalists. These meeting houses were scattered around Barrowford and as their membership grew they were able to erect their own small chapels before moving to larger premises – the Primitives and Congo's on Church Street and the Wesleyans at Higherford - or *'Canaan'* as it was better known.

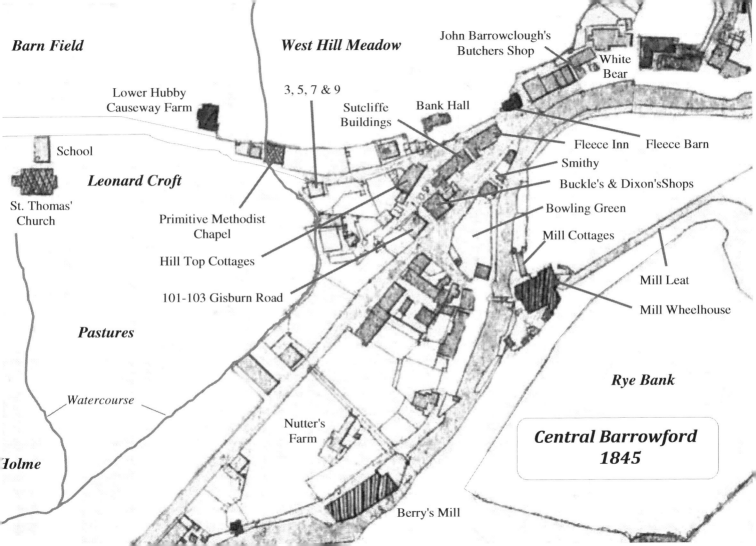

Barn Field

Lower Hubby
Causeway Farm

School

Leonard Croft

St. Thomas'
Church

Primitive Methodist
Chapel

Hill Top Cottages

101-103 Gisburn Road

Pastures

Watercourse

Holme

West Hill Meadow

3, 5, 7 & 9

Sutcliffe
Buildings

Bank Hall

John Barrowclough's
Butchers Shop

White
Bear

Fleece Inn   Fleece Barn

Smithy

Buckle's & Dixon'sShops

Bowling Green

Mill Cottages

Mill Leat

Mill Wheelhouse

Rye Bank

Nutter's
Farm

Berry's Mill

*Central Barrowford
1845*

Sutcliffe Buildings

The next row of buildings above John Totty's shop (fronting onto the turnpike road) were an assortment of three and four storey commercial premises. The first building was erected in the later eighteenth century, probably as a loom shop, and projected a long way out into the main road – so much so, in fact, that it had to be demolished as the new turnpike became established.

The most impressive property on this row was the four storey Sutcliffe Buildings which was originally a dandy shop built by the Sutcliffe family, who owned nearby Bank Hall along with land and property in the Halstead Lane area. This building became the headquarters of the Barrowford Industrial Co-operative Society when the premises were adapted for the purpose in 1852. Prior to this the Co-op was situated in the Square (where it had been originally founded sometime before 1847) before moving a few yards along to Stansfield Buildings at number 98 Gisburn Road and then across the road into the Sutcliffe Buildings.

The Co-op remained in the Sutcliffe Buildings for 57 years until it was decided to demolish the property and erect a brand new, purpose built store with public rooms in its place. In July 1909 work commenced on the demolition and the tradesmen who were to erect the new building were named as: Messrs. Dents (masonry) - Mr. Holgate of Wheatley Lane (joinery) - Nelson Co-op (plumbing) - Ormerods (slating) - Mr. Hartley of Colne (painting) - Mr. E. Butler of Barrowford (plastering).

The Co-op Row: c.1930

The 'new Co-op' is the building with the blinds outside and the Fleece Inn stands on the far side. The buildings to the left of the Co-op served many purposes over the years – the smaller one housed Hartley's Toffee Works in the later nineteenth century and Tom Lowcock was a boot and shoe maker here in the early twentieth century. These properties were demolished in 1933 in order to widen Gisburn Road, a bus lay-by and rose garden now occupy the site. Behind the Fleece Inn the Albert Mills dominate the area from their prominent position on West Hill.

Before this area of Barrowford, to the north of the highway, began to expand (in the later eighteenth century) the land hereabouts was largely owned by the Nowell, Sutcliffe and Hargreaves families. The Nowell estate fell into the hands of a landowning family named Farrington, of Leyland, through marriage and this is illustrated by a deed of 1889 showing that Henry Nowell Farrington Esq. had the title to the Fleece Inn plus a stable on the west side of Church street. In 1904 the Farringtons sold the; *'Fleece Inn, stable, shippon, slaughter house and other outbuildings belonging, and all closes of land thereto called Barn Fold, Stack Fearne, South and North West Hill Meadows and West Hill Field at 6 acres: 1 rood: 34 perches formerly occupied by James Hartley as tenant.'*

The Co-op Row: 1904-1909

This is the same row of properties as in the previous picture but viewed from the other end of the block. The Fleece Inn is on the extreme right with the Sutcliffe Buildings next door (stone steps running up the gable end). The tram lines were laid in 1903 and the Sutcliffe Buildings were demolished in 1909 thus providing us with a reasonably accurate date for the photograph.

The buildings on the extreme left are numbers 98-122 Gisburn Road and were erected on Bank Hall land (formerly the site of a blacksmiths shop and a lime kiln) which Oddie Sutcliffe, of Bank Hall, sold in 1840 to James Armistead for the erection of two cottages and a smithy - the sale also included an area of land measuring 60 feet in length along Gisburn Road by 35 feet in width on the Old Row side by 13 feet in width at the gable end - seen extreme left in the photograph.

In 1945 Bertha Horsley, spinster of 2 West Hill, bought all of the above (except the lock-up - the site of the smithy) along with two lock-up shops and houses being numbers 118, 120, 122.

Central Barrowford: 1904-09

In 1890 the shop at number 122 (with the lace curtains) was occupied by James Singleton, in 1893 William Booth occupied it and he was followed by George Dobney who was there in 1899 - these were all greengrocers. James Astin was a confectioner there in 1924, J. Blamiar was a florist there in 1941 and the above Miss Bertha Horsley was a draper in 1949. In 1964 the trustees of Bertha Horsley sold the property to Elizabeth Ann Dennison who ran it as a sweet shop. The former Post Office at number 110 was run as a boot and shoe makers and milliners by Jonas and Mrs. A. Sharp from 1890 to 1941.

GISBURN RD BARROWFORD.

On the extreme left of the photograph can be seen the frontages of Water Street and the gable of a row of houses on the Bowling Green. This latter area had once been an area of open land and served as the closest thing that Barrowford has ever had to a village green. Here the old and the young would congregate to play bowls or to sit around and catch up on the latest local gossip. The Stansfield brothers (Jonathan built Blacko Tower in 1890) erected the corner shop properties of 98 -102 Gisburn Road; the Bowling Green was gradually enclosed by other buildings and fell out of use. Many of the shops and cottages in this area were owned by members of the Nutter family, the butchery being run by them for many years.

Water Street (now River Way) ran from Gisburn Road, past the Bowling Green to the river and the properties on either side were built on land belonging to the Hargreaves family - Water Street was called Hargreaves Street for a number of years before reverting back to its original name.

Church Street: 1935-36

Taken in 1935-36 the photograph shows the site of the Fleece Inn (extreme left) shortly after demolition – a toilet block now occupies the site.

In the early nineteenth century Ellen Barrowclough ran the Fleece which was one of the principal Barrowford inns. Many meetings of the great and the good within the village were held within its walls along with Coroner's inquests. The inn brewed its own ale and the landlords farmed the 6 acres of local land belonging to the property; when the Farringtons took over in the later part of the nineteenth century the Fleece also farmed a number of acres at Newbridge. The photograph shows a bus outside the Lamb Club below which were originally the inn stables that had now become 'Sam O' Nicks' welding and engineering works. Here Lee Jackson and his son, Nicholas, made their own acetylene gas for welding from chips of calcium carbide and they also charged accumulators for domestic battery radios. Here glass-cased batteries were banked for charging by a paraffin-gas generator with a number of lamps inter-connected to lower the voltage.

The Fleece Inn: c.1915

By 1841 John Hartley (45) was running the Fleece Inn and farming the land along with his wife Mary (40) and 4 children – James Brown (30), the village constable, was lodging with the family at this time. The census of 1851 shows that Mary Ann Heap (23 – née Greenwood), a widow who had been born in Blackburn, was the innkeeper and was living with her 2 month-old daughter Nancy, her brother Ralph Greenwood (25) who was a servant at the inn, and Mary Slater (19) of Manchester, also a servant. Lodging at the inn were Thomas Whitaker (51), a blacksmith who would be followed in this trade by other Whitakers in the village, and Ormerod Barrowclough (28) an unmarried cotton manufacturer from Barrowford – it is likely that the Barrowcloughs still held the main tenancy of the inn at this time.

By 1861 the inn had been taken over by Ellis Fell (46), from Roughlee, and his wife Ann (37), from Barley. Their 15 year-old son, Edward, was a trainee teacher and there were 4 other children. Ten years later Ellis and Ann were still at the Fleece and Edward had now become a schoolmaster. In 1881 things had changed little as we find Ellis and Ann still running the establishment along with daughter Mary (24) who was a barmaid. Sons James (30) and John (20) were still living with their parents and were both weavers. Another son, Edward (35) lived nearby at Bank Hall with his wife Hannah (38), from Fence, and daughter Alice (1). Edward (previously the farm-hand at Trough Laithe Farm) was an assistant innkeeper and farmer, working for his father at the Fleece; by 1896 he had taken over as the licensee.

Ellis and Ann Fell had another son, also named Ellis who was probably their eldest and the London edition of the *Illustrated Police News* reported on Saturday March 1st 1890 that:

A shocking discovery was made on Saturday evening last (23rd February) at the foot of Pendle Hill in Lancashire. A man named Ellis Fell, aged 50 of Barrowford, was found by a farmer lying dead in a field with his head fearfully crushed, the farmer being attracted to the spot by the piteous howling of the deceased's dog. No foul-play is suspected, no robbery had been attempted and there were no signs of a struggle. The man had not shot himself as his gun was found lying near, still loaded. The police believe that the deceased, in getting over a stone wall, slipped and fell against the wall; the stones dropping on his head inflicted fatal injuries.

Ellis lived in the row of cottages between the Old Row and the main road, where we earlier met with John Emmott - this tragic accident left Ellis's widow, Betty, with 4 children to support.

Sam O' Nicks: 1935-6

We have seen that the building that became Sam O' Nicks (Jackson's) engineering shop was the barn and stables belonging to the Fleece Inn; this building was described in 1827 as a new barn belonging to widow Barrowclough. She was the wife of John Barrowclough and mother of John Barrowclough who founded a cotton manufacturing dynasty in Barrowford that was to last for a hundred years. It is time, then, to meet this family.

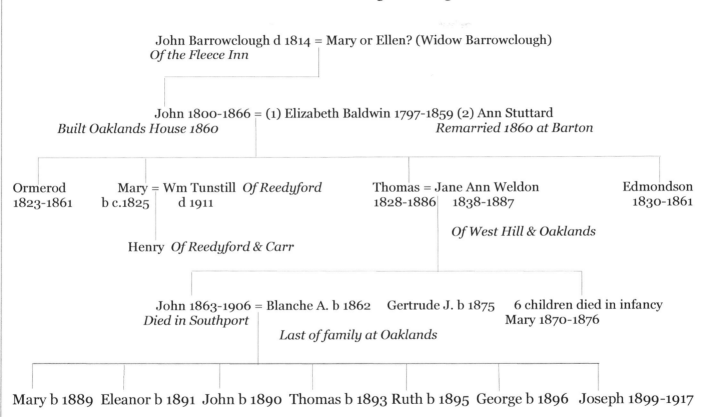

The Barrowclough Family

John Barrowclough d 1814 = Mary or Ellen? (Widow Barrowclough)
Of the Fleece Inn

John 1800-1866 = (1) Elizabeth Baldwin 1797-1859 (2) Ann Stuttard
Built Oaklands House 1860   *Remarried 1860 at Barton*

Ormerod   Mary = Wm Tunstill *Of Reedyford*   Thomas = Jane Ann Weldon   Edmondson
1823-1861   b c.1825   d 1911   1828-1886   1838-1887   1830-1861

                                                          Of West Hill & Oaklands

        Henry *Of Reedyford & Carr*

John 1863-1906 = Blanche A. b 1862   Gertrude J. b 1875   6 children died in infancy
Died in Southport   Mary 1870-1876
                        Last of family at Oaklands

Mary b 1889 Eleanor b 1891 John b 1890 Thomas b 1893 Ruth b 1895 George b 1896 Joseph 1899-1917

John Barrowclough's Shop and House

The small building with smoke coming from the chimney was John Barrowclough's butchers shop. To the left stands the house in which he lived and to the right is the druggists shop at 137 Gisburn Road

The first John Barrowclough in Barrowford was born around the middle of the eighteenth century and, by the earlier part of the nineteenth century he and his wife were running the Fleece Inn along with its farming and butchery operation. Their son, John, was born in 1800-01 and he inherited his father's business acumen to the extent that he was famed for taking a very careful approach to his money. John junior tried his hand at a number of money-making schemes; he helped his parents with the butchery business as well as hawking for a village baker. The family owned and ran the small butchers shop in the West Hill buildings.

By the early 1840s, having accumulated enough money, John took the tenancy of Bogmoriles Mill which stood at the top of David Street (approximately where Prospect Terrace now stands). Built by the Sutcliffe brothers Bogmoriles was an early example of a steam powered mill with 200 looms on two floors. However, the rather precarious position of the mill on a steep embankment, with a limited water supply, meant that it fell into disuse and, by about 1860, had become derelict. Around the year 1852 Barrowclough had become wealthy enough to build his own mill and he erected Park Mill and Shed at the bottom of Halstead lane, a short distance from Bogmoriles Mill.

Park Shed: 2008

Sometime around 1820 John Barrowclough married Elizabeth Baldwin, daughter of local manufacturer Ormerod Baldwin. In the eighteenth century the Baldwins had been a weaving family within the Colne district, a branch of whom ran the Cross Gates Inn at Blacko during the latter half of the eighteenth century and were closely related to the Ormerod family. In the late 1700s Ormerod Baldwin occupied the two properties at West Hill that would become 129 and 131 Gisburn Road. Baldwin's dwelling at number 129 was known as the Size House and 131 was Baldwin's warehouse.

West Hill Row
Left to right: 125 and 127 Gisburn Road
129: The Size House
131: Baldwin's Warehouse

The Size House was probably built in the 1790s and its purpose was to serve the local handloom weavers who brought their warps here to have them sized with a mixture based on animal tallow. Sizing the warp strengthened the threads and made weaving easier by reducing friction.

Size was also used to increase the weight of the woven cloth by unscrupulous weavers who would apply an excess – unfortunately this led to the cloth going mouldy which imparted a glossy finish to it. Those who practised this deceit were known as *'Mould Heels'* and an example of this can be seen in the Pendle Witch trials of 1612 where Katherine Hewitt (Old Mould Heels), wife of John Hewitt, a clothier from Colne, was a friend of Elizabeth Southern (OldDemdike)of Blacko.

Thomas Barrowclough

Between them the Baldwins and Barrowcloughs owned the West Hill area running from the Fleece Inn along to the White Bear and stretching back into West Hill Field on the hill to the rear. The size house was the first of the extant West Hill buildings to be erected followed by the warehouse next door. By 1840 John Barrowclough had upgraded the warehouse into living accommodation by the addition of a new frontage and was living here with his wife Elizabeth, sons Ormerod, Thomas and Edmondson and daughter Mary.

Around 1840 Barrowclough erected the properties of 125 and 127 Gisburn Road on land owned by his widowed mother containing an old joiners shop, an old barn and a warehouse. She also owned a close of land called West Hill to the north on which were erected two cottages – probably the two West Hill Cottages set back from the main road (135-137). All the houses on West Hill, with the exception of Baldwin's and Barrowclough's houses, were built for multi-occupation where there were cellar dwellings to the front of 125-127, along with dwellings to the rear, and dwellings to the rear of West Hill Cottages.

All the back cottages were accessed by a road which ran up the side and along the back of 125 almost to the White Bear.

West Hill Cottages
L to R: Barrowclough's Butchers Shop
2 & 4 West Hill (West Hill Cottages)
Druggists Shop (137 Gisburn Road)

In the later 1900s West Hill Cottages and number 125 Gisburn Road were owned by Henry Baldwin (who had been the Greave of Pendle Forest for 11 years) who left them in 1896 to his daughter, Ann Roberts, of 33 Church Street - her husband William owned other properties on Church Street. In 1902 Ann Roberts conveyed her estate to her husband and James and Arthur Armistead Bracewell; the estate was described as:

'3 houses with cellars on Gisburn Road and 2 and 4 West Hill bounded on the north by a back street, on the south by the turnpike road, on the east by a double house and on the west by a side street.'

125 (left) to 127 Gisburn Road and the Size House

The shop at 137 Gisburn Road was a druggists and Post Office run for a number of years in the later nineteenth century by Thomas Nowell, uncle to Fred Nowell who shot

his wife on Dixon Street in 1897. The shop was owned by John Barrowclough who sold it for £250 in 1905 – the Swinglehurts ran it as a chemists shop in the 1920s and 30s.

Oaklands House

Of John Barrowclough's children it was to be Thomas who inherited the family flair for business and he joined his father in partnership at Park Shed. However, this business relationship was dissolved in February 1863, three years before John died. Already a part of a family who had married into land and property Thomas Barrowclough consolidated this by marrying Jane Ann Weldon around 1861. Jane was the daughter of Rev. R S Weldon, of Wexford, and Elizabeth who was the sister of John Holt. John was of the Parker-Swinglehurst-Holt families who owned a great deal of land in Barrowford and the surrounding district, the main estate being centred on Park Hill – he later occupied Grove House.

Thomas never looked back; he was born into manufacturing and he was to die in it. By 1861 he was living in his parent's old house at West Hill where he was described as a *master cotton spinner*. Also here were his wife Jane Ann (23), household servant Jane Barnes (27), of Grindleton, and chambermaid Alice Hanson (19), of Downham. In the August of that same year the Preston Guardian ran the following report:

Colne Court – Thomas Barrowclough, of Barrowford, took an action against Robert Bradshaw, of Colne. Some time ago Mr Barrowclough and Bradshaw's employer were in company together at the George and Dragon, Barrowford. They laid a wager of £12 each as to who was worth the most money. The defendant (Bradshaw) was the stake-holder and as the dispute was never settled he has had possession of the money ever since. In court Bradshaw acknowledged that he had made away with the money but that he had been compelled to do so under a series of unfortunate circumstances. Bradshaw was ordered to repay the £12 to Barrowclough or face 40 days in prison by default.

Two years previously John Barrowclough had bought land from the Grimshaws across from St. Thomas' church known as Hubbycourse Meadow and Barn Field. This area adjoined the family land at West Hill and here John built his new mansion house of Oaklands. Unfortunately John's wife died in 1859 while the house was in the process of construction and she never saw it finished. Within a matter of months John had remarried to Ann Stuttard, of Higham, but the marriage took place in Barton-upon-Irwell near Manchester. This begs the question as to whether John deliberately married well out of the way of the village gossips, seeing that he appears to have taken a new wife with what would have been viewed at that time as undue haste.

Oaklands Lodge

In 1861 John Barrowclough (60) appeared on the census at Oaklands along with his new wife, Ann (55) and a visitor named Mary Meredith (20), from Manchester. There was one servant at the house in the form of Jane Broughton (21), from Thornton in Yorkshire. By the time of the 1871 census John had died and his wife appears to have moved out of Barrowford; living at Oaklands now we find John's son Thomas (43), his wife Jane Ann (33), son John (8) and daughter Mary (2). Tragically the following years were not happy ones for the family as Mary was destined to live only four more years. In 1878 Thomas and Jane had a son, Thomas, who lived for 29 weeks and another five children born to the couple died in infancy. Also at Oaklands in 1871 were Jane Barnes (38), the cook who had been with Thomas and Jane at West Hill, Ellen [?] (24), from Grindleton was the nursemaid, Ruth Farer (21), from Manchester the nurse and Jonas Laycock (47), from Kildwick, was the footman.

In 1881 Thomas and Jane Barrowclough were still at Oaklands although Jane was not at home on the day that the census was taken. Thomas (53) was described as a *cotton manufacturer employing 750 hands and a farmer of 53 acres* while son John (18) was a *cotton spinner and manufacturer*. Daughter Gertrude Jane (6) was a scholar and servants at the house were Henry Whittle (21), the coachman from Hereford, Ellen Swift (23), a domestic servant from Manchester, Sarah Barnes (22), a chambermaid from Liverpool, Ann Christian (45), a cook from the Isle of Man and Ellen Kin (21), a nurse from Stratford.

John Barrowclough 1863-1906

The Lodge House for the Oaklands estate stands directly opposite to the original St. Thomas' church on Church Street and resident here in 1881 were a family headed by Henry Hatton (33), a gardener from Childwall along with his wife Dorothy (30), from Liverpool and 4 children. Also resident here is Amos Hartley (20), an assistant gardener born in Barrowford.

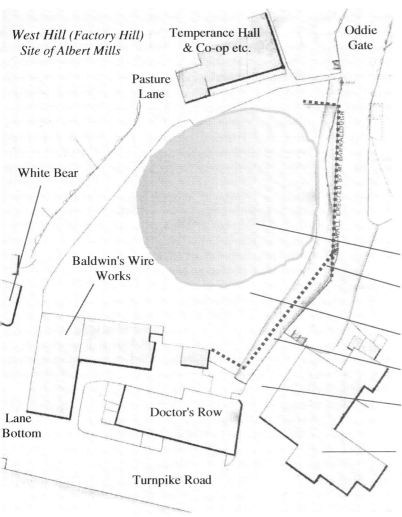

West Hill (Factory Hill)
Site of Albert Mills

Temperance Hall
& Co-op etc.

Oddie Gate

Pasture Lane

White Bear

Baldwin's Wire Works

Lane Bottom

Doctor's Row

Turnpike Road

WALL ERECTED BY MR BARROWCLOUGH

By now we see that Thomas and Jane's son, John, had joined his father in cotton manufacturing. However, John appears to have been typical of the 'third generation syndrome' where the grandson has little interest in running the long established family firm - certainly by the time that John had become involved the business was a force to be reckoned with. To understand this we must go back to 1804 when William Bannister, a *'yeoman late of Barrowford'* left properties and land in his will.

Barrowclough's Mill Site: 1849

Lodge (filled in by 1820)

Wall erected by John Barrowclough in 1849 to enclose his new mill site

The Crofts (orchard and garden areas)

Deep Clough

Occupation Lane (Halstead Lane) to Halstead's Farm, Oddie Sutcliffe's Farm & Higher Ridge

Slaughterhouse, Blacksmiths shop, Warping Shop, Oddies Barn and Cottages

In a tortuous descent of property over the centuries the land at the bottom of Halstead Lane passed through the hands of those who owned the Park Hill estate. This area was known as Charles Farm and became detached from Park Hill within the mists of time, being partly retained by the Bannister family, erstwhile owners of Park Hill. In 1804 William Bannister left a number of cottages, workshops, shops and land at the bottom of Halstead Lane (or Occupation Lane as it was then) in trust to Christopher Sutcliffe, a mason and a member of a local family of landowners, who duly acquired the property in 1828 on payment of a fine of 5 shillings. An indenture was created to the effect that Christopher Sutcliffe and his wife, Jenny, would rent out the properties for a sum of £2 per annum to blacksmith John Pollard and Charles Bannister. By 1846 both Christopher Sutcliffe and Charles Bannister had died leaving an outstanding mortgage on the properties of £350 plus interest. Samuel Turner was the trustee of the properties and duly advertised them to be sold at the Golden Fleece Inn, Barrowford on the 9th of October 1848.

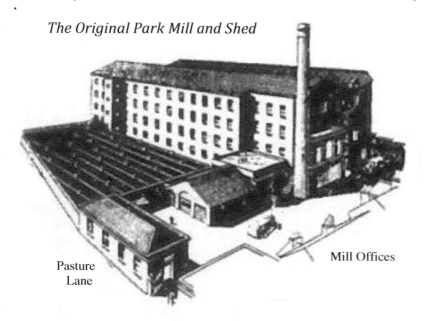

The Original Park Mill and Shed

Pasture Lane

Mill Offices

The auction properties covered most of the buildings and land illustrated on the previous page. These were tenanted at the time by Oddie Sutcliffe of Bank Hall who sub-let the Crofts to James Robinson who occupied them as an orchard and gardens. John Barrowclough purchased Lot 1 and Lot 2 for £200 and £250 respectively but, for some reason he allowed Jonas Edmondson, a local blacksmith, to buy Lot 3 at £134 while William Spencer, a weaver, bought Lot 6 at £88. Subsequent to the sale Barrowclough purchased Edmondson and Spencer's Lots from them at the price they had paid for them – somewhere behind this lies a story!

Having purchased most of the land he required for his new mill John Barrowclough began to wall of his property and to evict the tenants from the buildings. Finally, in 1852, the last piece of the jigsaw fell into place when deeds show that he purchased the last remaining parcels of the two Crofts from a Clitheroe cotton manufacturer named Atacer [*sic.*] along with the land and buildings on *'Factory Hill.'* This latter was the site of Albert Mills, behind the White Bear, and this suggests that a building of some kind already existed here when Barrowclough bought the land in 1852.

Over the period 1853-56 Barrowclough erected his spinning operation of Park Mill at four storeys along with a single story weaving shed and, in 1856, he began work on building the Middle Mill of the Albert Mills complex – this was the imposing factory that was to loom over the White Bear and West Hill for over a century.

Albert Mills from Rye Bank: 1965

A protracted series of extensions meant that by 1885 the Albert Mills ran 53,736 weft and twist spindles and 1,501 looms. In 1880 the imposing building that was to become the Council Offices was built as the offices for Albert Mills. We have seen that John Barrowclough junior had little interest in the family business and following his father Thomas' death in 1886 he ran the mills for less than five years, selling the business to coal merchant James Aitken of Spring Grove, Higher Park Hill, in 1891. The mills were subsequently occupied by a number of small manufacturing concerns until being partly demolished in the 1960s.

John Barrowclough, then, had little interest in the business built by his father and grandfather but, in mitigation, it has to be said that he came into the family firm at a time when the cotton trade was going through one of its many periods of protracted depression. The following press cuttings illustrate the mood within the trade at that time:

Aberdeen Weekly Journal: June 16th 1877: *Yesterday morning 1,000 weavers recently employed at the mill of Mr Barrowclough, Barrowford, returned to work on being promised a slight increase in wages. The cotton trade is much depressed; the spinning branch has never been known to be more depressed.*

Leeds Mercury: April 1878: *80% - 90% of looms stopped in Burnley and at Padiham only one mill is working. A crowd of 4,000 people there burnt an effigy of the mill master. At Barrowford Mr Barrowclough's workforce are all on strike. Yesterday morning (Thursday April 18th) the mills were ready to start had the operatives accepted the pay reduction, but they did not do so.*

Bristol Mercury: October 28th 1878: *The depression in trade within Lancashire is extreme. Danes House Mill, Burnley, has stopped for a month and Gannow Mill is stopping 30,000 spindles as they can buy yarns much cheaper than they can spin them. There are many redundancies in the iron-founding trade. Mr Keighley and Mr Bracewell have had to lay off 50 men and Messrs Butterworth and Dickinson have given notice of wage reductions from 5% up. Mr Barrowclough, cotton spinner and manufacturer, has commenced short time of 28 hours per week.*

Manchester Times: July 12th 1879: *Mr Thomas Barrowclough, of Barrowford, has given notice that in consequence of the severe depression in the cotton industry he will stop his mills after the cotton is worked out. The state of the trade has never presented a more gloomy face than it does now.*

Leeds Mercury: January 24th 1885: *Messrs Berry Brothers of Barrowford have given notice to the weavers in their employ of their intentions to reduce wages by 5%. The firm runs about 1,000 looms and the notice will affect about 350 hands. Last week Mr Barrowclough gave notice of a similar reduction. Mr Barrowclough is the largest employer of labour in the immediate area and the combined reduction will affect over 1,000 hands. There is every reason to believe that the proposal will be accepted by the operatives.*

Manchester Times: February 20th 1886: *Mr. Thomas Barrowclough and Messrs Wiseman and Smith* (Higherford Mill) *of Barrowford have agreed to an advance in the weavers wages to the extent of 5%.*

Manchester Times: Saturday July 30th 1887: *The operatives at the factory of Mr Thomas Barrowclough and Sons, Barrowford, have struck work owing to a wages dispute.*

The Barrowclough Memorial and Vault (St. Thomas' Churchyard)

Whatever John's reasons were for losing interest in the business it is clear that he had not suffered unduly from the vagaries of the cotton trade. In 1901 we find him as master of the house at Oaklands and, whereas his father had employed 5 household servants in 1881, the family were now served by at least 10 members of household staff. John had married a Suffolk girl named Blanche around 1879 and over the following years he was to spend an increasing amount of time at his favourite resort of Southport where he had purchased a property. The family divided their lives between Barrowford and Southport, two of John and Blanche's 7 children being born there in 1895 and 1896. At Oaklands, in 1901, were John Barrowclough (38), cotton manufacturer, his wife Blanche A (39) and children Mary (12), Eleanor (10), John (9), Thomas (8), Ruth, (6), George (5) and Joseph (2).

Serving at Oaklands House in 1901 were Mary Saxby (39), a governess from Kent, Isabella Wilson (38), a parlour maid from Morecambe, Isabella Barclay (26), a housemaid from Scotland, Frances Clarke (22), another housemaid from Cheshire, Annie Bennett (26), a laundry maid from Lincolnshire, Sarah Robinson (24), also a laundry maid from Southport, Bertha England (22), a kitchen maid from Addingham, Maggie Gurbett (20), a nurse maid from Shropshire and Amelia Mickleburgh (48), the children's nurse from Norfolk. At the lodge were James Tattersall (44), the coachman from Rawtenstall, his wife Elizabeth (42), from Todmorden, daughter Susannah (22), a school mistress and 6 other children.

Shortly before his death at Morecambe in 1906 John Barrowclough sold off the Oaklands House estate comprising the house and 3 farms for the sum of £17,000 to James Ridehalgh JP (1867-1936) a cotton manufacture in Nelson and at Lower Clough Mill in Barrowford. James' son, James (of West Hill Cottages), married Elizabeth Lonsdale and their son, John Ridehalgh, ran Higherford Mill. Oaklands was sold again in 1941 for the sum of £6,650 when it became the N.F.S headquarters for billets and offices.

Oaklands House Lodge Gates: c.1915

Thomas Barrowclough was a generous benefactor to St. Thomas' church which stood opposite the entrance to Oaklands House. He once invited the church choir to a dinner at the house and his wife, when showing the group around the house, opened a cupboard to reveal a large number of rusty old clog-irons. These, she explained, had been collected from the roadside many years ago by Thomas' father, John Barrowclough, who insisted that they should never be thrown away as *'they would come in handy one day.'* On one occasion John had been laying down the law to some of his workers at the mill when one of the older women said to him; *'Tha's not hawkin' muffins now with thi' trouser 'arse hanging out!'* This reflected John's early struggle to accumulate enough money to set up in business.   Thomas' brother, Ormerod, lived at the Fleece Inn for many years and he was not renowned for his subtle manner. He courted a local girl for a while and decided to propose to her by letter which read; *'Not that I could not do better – both in beauty, tin* (money) *and other matters . . .'* --- The lady did not marry him!

The last John Barrowclough, son of Thomas, does not appear to have been as hard-headed in business as his grandfather, John, had been. In June 1890 the death of Doctor de Beeho Pim was reported somewhat

prematurely as, although he had been ill, he was still very much alive. On hearing of Dr. Pim's illness John Barrowclough ordered that the looms at Park Shed should stop running until he recovered. This was due to the fact that the Doctor lived at 147 Gisburn Road (Doctor's Row) and his bedroom overlooked directly onto the weaving shed. Barrowclough obviously considered that the noise of the looms would delay the Doctor's recovery and it must be said that the voluntary stoppage would have cost the business a substantial amount of money.

Albert Mills Offices
(Site of Doctor's Row)

James and Robert Hayhurst: 1949

Outside James' home at Oaklands House with Robert's Rolls Royce

Mr. T Hayhurst was a successful butcher in Nelson and lived at Park House on Walton Lane. His sons, James and Robert, were to make their mark within the local community – James became a chemist and druggist in Nelson while Robert toured the world with his motorcycle stunt show better known as the wall-of-death.

When he was not touring with his show Robert cut a dapper figure as he roared around the local highways and byways in his 1930s MG sports car. He took his show to places as diverse as New York, Germany and Russia where his daredevil antics proved to be highly popular with the crowds. Russia, in fact, was to prove to be the nemesis of his touring days as he fell foul of the Stalin regime. He had taken the show across from Germany where he had engaged a German stunt rider to work with him but unfortunately the Russian authorities found out that his new partner was the brother of a German SS officer. This being the time running up to WWII the weight of officialdom came down heavily upon Robert and his co-rider – the wall-of-death equipment, including their Douglas 600cc motorcycles, was impounded and the two unfortunates were informed that they were to be detained.

In the end Robert managed to make it out of Russia, leaving his belongings behind, and shortly after his arrival back in England, he found himself in the army as, appropriately enough, a motorcycle dispatch rider working with Sir Malcolm Campbell.

The Bottom of Oaklands Drive
The extant gate posts framing St. Thomas' tower

Following the War James Hayhurst, who ran a prospering chemist business at premises on Railway Street and (later) Market Street in Nelson, purchased the Oaklands House estate and, as we have seen, Clough Farm. He had a son, Robert, who followed his father into the profession of chemist and druggist, and his daughter, Janet, followed a career in the nursing profession. At Oaklands, James began to breed Hackney carriage horses and he produced a number of high class animals. One of these sold for a handsome sum to a Texas oil multi-millionaire, the only drawback being that part of the deal involved James' stable groom going to live in Texas along with the horse. The horse breeding took James and son Robert to the Buckingham Palace stables on one occasion where they were amazed to see that the ornate cast iron stalls were identical to those installed at the Oaklands stables.

James' son Robert carried on the family chemist business and his skills as a photographer were put to good use in the other family concern of Hayhurst's Camera Shop. Robert recalls many interesting stories from family life at Oaklands, not least of which revolve around his Uncle Robert's adventures. Following his army demob Uncle Robert used his keen business eye and saw an opportunity in the army surplus market. He traded in a large variety of ex-military hardware but his main passion was that of motor vehicles (the Rolls Royce on the previous page being an example). On one occasion Robert's nephew, Robert, remembers his uncle arriving at Oaklands House in a wagon on which he was carrying 10,000 brand-new surplus bedpans – it was fortunate that Robert and his father were retail chemists and were eventually able to sell all of the 'guzunders' thus averting a local glut in the bedpan market!

The White Bear Inn: 1950s
With the Albert Mills behind; this was John Barrowclough's Middle Mill of 1853-56

The White Bear Inn is one of the finest houses of its type in the area and stands as testament to a period when local farmers began to emerge from the obscurity of tenantry into a world where they would be regarded as wealthy yeomen. In all probability the building was erected in 1667 by James Hargreaves of Water Meetings Farm although a datestone carries the date of 1607.

In July of 1652 John Bannister of Park Hill borrowed the sum of £200, at an interest rate of 8%, from Henry Hargreaves. Henry was a wealthy clothier of Water Meetings who had accumulated wealth and land through his dealings as a *'putter-out'* or cloth merchant who acted as a local bank by lending other business people money in the form of mortgages. Henry was obviously a hard-headed business man as John Bannister described him as; *'A very hard, oppressing and vigorous man.'* When Henry died in 1658 he was still owed money by the Bannister family (erstwhile owners of the area upon which Henry's son, James, built his Great House) and it is possible that the land was gained through default on this loan.

Water Meetings Farm
Home of the Hargreaves family
from at least the early 16ᵗʰ century

Henry Hargreaves died in 1658 and his main properties passed through the line of James, one of his 6 children. It was this line of descent who built the White Bear which, at the time of building, was known as Hargreaves Great House. The building was erected on the site of Charles Farm at Lane Bottom, this was the area of land between the bottom of Pasture Lane and the White Bear, later to be known as Bracewell Hill.

In a 1713 inventory of yeoman's houses James Hargreaves is listed for the Great House, as is his son, John – James is also listed for the Water Meetings Farm which was rented out to George Hartley who farmed it. The farm buildings belonging to the Great House stood to the east while the barn appears to have been higher up the hill at Green Bank. Situated in the two Crofts across Pasture Lane was an old barn that was still standing when John Barrowclough bought the land in the later 1840s – at this time it was occupied by Oddie Sutcliffe of Bank Hall. Sometime during the earlier eighteenth century a part of the Great House was used as a beer house, this was also the case with many other roadside farms where an increase in the cotton trade led to an increase in traffic and, therefore, a demand for hospitality. By the 1770s the house was being described as both Hargreaves Great House and the White Bear.

The White Bear: c.1933
In this photograph the bridge to the park is opposite the inn porch whereas now it stands some 50 metres higher upstream

The inventory of John Hargreaves' will (dated 1713) lists; *The Great House (the house body) – great parlour (SE room) – kitchen (SW room) – milkhouse and wash house (NW wing?) – little parlour (NE wing?) and detached loom shop – chambers over the house, parlour, kitchen, porch, little parlour and milkhouse.* An earlier inventory of 1687 makes no mention of a little parlour or wash house and this might be due to the fact that either the building was not finished at this time or John, who lived with his widowed father James, did not occupy all of the house.

A branch of the Hargreaves family married into the Barrowford Laund estate and from this line came Abraham Hargreaves who converted the old Barrowford Mill to a cotton spinning concern in the later 1700s - by 1803 Abraham had inherited the Great House which is described as *Charles Farm, public house and brew house.* Charles Farm was occupied at this time by John Bracewell who gave his name to Bracewell Hill.

By 1841 John Bracewell's widow, Nancy (50), from Barrowford, was running the White Bear Inn along with her daughter Jennet (25); also living here were Hannah (13) and Joseph Sutcliffe (9) and John Mills (7). The following national census of 1851 shows that Nancy Bracewell was still the landlady and was assisted by her daughter Jennet (37). Also living at the inn was Jennet's daughter Janet (4) and Nancy's nephew, John Sutcliffe (15), who was described as a servant.

In 1861 Richard Woodworth (37), from Long Preston, was the innkeeper and farmer of 13 acres at the White Bear which he occupied with his wife Jane (41), from Goldshaw Booth and children William (11), Robert (8), James (6), Mary A. (4) and John (1). The farm labourer was Richard's cousin, Nathan Clarke (25), of Long Preston. Richard and Jane would go on to keep another local inn, the Bay Horse at Roughlee, and they also kept a farm house known as The Last Shift as a beer shop. The couple were hard-working, had 13 children and were nicknamed *'Dick in a minit and Jane in a crack.'*

By 1871 we find Jane (27) and Agnes Midgeley (25), from Brogden, are the innkeepers assisted by their sister Betsy Midgeley (23), from Barnoldswick, another sister, Mary A (19), from Barnoldswick, their uncle, Robert Parkinson (65), a retired cotton weaver from Lower Billington and their niece, Betsy (6), from Brogden.

In 1881 Betsy Midgeley (33) had taken over the inn from her sisters and was living there with her uncle Robert Parkinson (74), who had an income from cottages, and another relative, James Ridehalgh (38), from Barrowford was running the 14 acre farm. Other young relatives named Healar and Wright were living at the inn and Fanny Wright (19), from Birmingham, was the domestic servant. Betsy Midgeley carried on at the White bear for a number of years before retiring to a cottage in Nelson. By 1908 the landlord was James Almond, in 1911 Benjamin Taylor, in 1923 William Shorrocks, in 1933 A Clarkson and during the 1940s J. Frankland and A. Towler.

In 1964 we final year primary pupils were taken from Rushton Street School to the White Bear to see the large fireplace and the original doorway in the porch recently uncovered by building improvement works.

Barrowford Old Mill (Mill in the Park)

Where once echoed the monotonous crashing of water powered spinning frames there is little now to be heard other than the voices of children as they happily dash from one item of playground equipment to another. All that now remains of the ancient Old Mill is an embankment running across Barrowford park that once carried the water from the river upstream to power the water wheel and the remnant of a forlorn masonry wall buried within the steep slopes of Rye Bank.

There have been suggestions that the Old Mill can trace its lineage directly back to the period of the late thirteenth century, not long after the Norman Conquest, when the weather was clement, crops grew abundantly and the population grew. This meant that there was an increased demand for the local woollen products and facilities to grind the farmer's grain. Fulling mills sprang up on rivers that were powerful enough to drive the heavy wooden stocks that pounded the woven woollen pieces so as to mesh their fibres together. There is, unfortunately, no direct evidence to suggest that the Old Barrowford Mill was erected at this time as either a fulling mill or a corn mill. From 1311 records do exist for other such mills within Colne, Marsden and Burnley that prove our area played a part within the commercial output of the extended estate within which our locality fell – namely the Lordship of the Honour of Clitheroe.

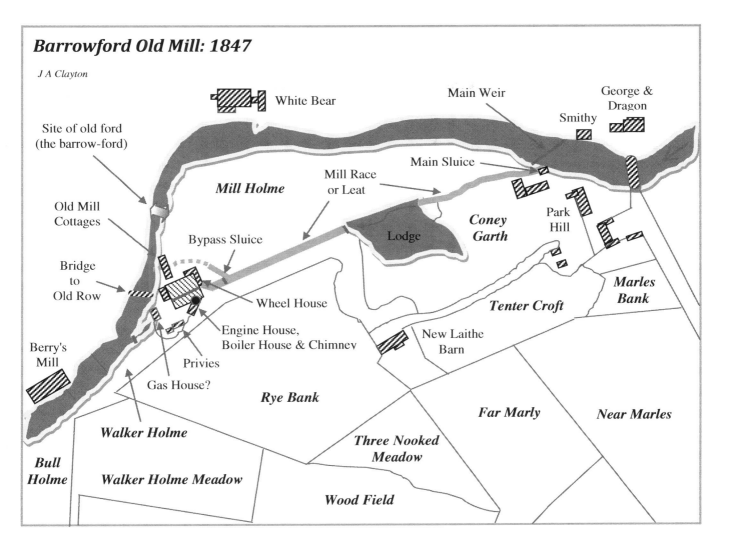

Barrowford Old Mill: 1847

J A Clayton

White Bear

Main Weir

George & Dragon

Smithy

Site of old ford
(the barrow-ford)

Main Sluice

Mill Holme

Mill Race
or Leat

Coney Garth

Park Hill

Old Mill Cottages

Lodge

Marles Bank

Bypass Sluice

Bridge to Old Row

Wheel House

Engine House, Boiler House & Chimney

Tenter Croft

New Laithe Barn

Berry's Mill

Privies

Gas House?

Rye Bank

Far Marly

Near Marles

Walker Holme

Three Nooked Meadow

Bull Holme

Walker Holme Meadow

Wood Field

Last Vestige of the Old Mill: 2009

Our first real clue as to the date of the Old Mill can be found within the records of the Clitheroe estate where a deposition of 1541 makes mention of a mill in Lower Barrowford situated *'where 4 common highways meet.'* At this time the old roads through Barrowford crossed close to the mill, the Back Lane (now Church Street) passed down the hill in front of Bank Hall to a ford in the river opposite the Fleece Inn and on to Colne via Park Hill - thus forming a cross-roads with the main Marsden to Gisburn road.

At this particular time the people of Pendle Forest (of which Barrowford was a part) submitted an official complaint that they had to travel too far to grind their corn, the nearest mills being at Bradley (Marsden – this mill was often out of service due to neglect), Colne and Foulridge. If there had been a tied corn mill at Barrowford it is probable that this complaint would not have arisen but it is possible that the Old Mill mainly served the grain producers on the extended Park Hill estate, the tenants of Park Hill being exempt from their duty of *'multure.'* This meant that they were not obligated to grind their corn at mills designated by the Clitheroe estate where profits were split between the Crown and the mill owners.

By the eighteenth century the Old Mill had been a corn grinding operation but when it was converted from its use as a fulling mill is unclear. The area now forming a trackway connecting the park (Mill Holme) and the playing fields (Bull Holme) was originally called *Walker Holme* while the adjoining meadow now occupied by allotments was called *Walker Holme Meadow*. The term *'walker'* was used in conjunction with the processing of woollens where the early method of fulling was for people to manually tread the worsted cloth in order to bind the warp and the weft into a finished cloth piece.

Millstone at Park Hill

Further to the textile production we also find that the field alongside the trackway from Park Hill up to the cemetery was known as *Tenter Field* – *'tenting'* being the act of pegging out fulled woollen pieces in fields to stretch and dry them. When other field-names around the area of the mill are examined there is a suggestion that they would have been named during the latter part of the fifteenth, and early sixteenth, centuries when there had been a push to take new lands into production. If this is indeed the case then there is an argument in the *Walker* and *Tenter* field-names for the Old Mill having been a textile operation from this time at least.

We saw earlier that John Bannister (1603-1654) of Park Hill borrowed the sum of £200 from Henry Hargreaves of Water Meetings – this sum translates into today's money (average earnings index) to £318,000 with a minimum annual repayment of £26,000. John's son Henry (1631-1682) married Elizabeth Shaw of Langroyd Hall in Colne and the Old Mill stayed within the family for the following two centuries. Their great-great grandson, Robert Bannister (1723-1780), of Colne Hall, left the mill in his will with the instructions to his trustees to obtain the best price they could for it. In consequence the mill (described as a *'cloth or fulling mill'*) was sold in 1783 to Abraham Hargreaves and his uncle, Christopher Hargreaves (d. 1812) for £233 and so began the most productive period within the long life of the Old Mill.

Abraham Hargreaves was the son of James Hargreaves (d. 1791) of Barrowford Laund who was a descendant of James, the builder of the White Bear. Here, then, we see the Hargreaves family had improved their lot over the period from AD1500-1800 while the long established gentry family of Bannister were in decline and losing their property to the now-established class of yeomanry.

The Main Sluice: Standing adjacent to the waterfall, or mill caul, this is all that remains of the system that directed water from the river to the lodge and subsequently to the mill water wheel

In 1784 Abraham Hargreaves (1744-1804), of Heirs House, kept a diary - this was then momentous year when Barrowford turned the corner from a hand-powered economy to that of a forward-looking mechanised modern age and the diary is a fascinating resource from that time.

In the period of Abraham's acquisition of the Old Mill it was common for the old corn mill owners to convert their mills to textile work. In this way some of the great textile pioneers of the district made their fortunes, these included Nicholas England, Robert Shaw and John Phillips of Colne. Abraham was slightly different in that he purchased a mill with the sole intention of converting it to spinning and in this he needed expert help. He enlisted the aid of his friend, John Greenwood of Keighley, who oversaw the complex operation of installing the new cotton spinning frames and trained Abraham in their operation. Greenwood was also a manufacturer of spinning machinery and Abraham's diary notes deliveries of new machines from Keighley every Wednesday.

Abraham was a farmer and dealer in malt and this is probably how he came to acquire the Old Mill. His trade would also have brought him directly into contact with Thomas Grimshaw who was also a maltster. Grimshaw had some kind of input into Abraham's spinning venture and he passed on his knowledge of spinning to his sons, Christopher and James Grimshaw who went on to build the Higherford Mill in 1824.

The Old Mill: c.1830-32

The photograph shows the building of Abraham Hargreaves' time when he had converted it on the principal of the Arkwright mill system

In 1800 Abraham and Christopher Hargreaves purchased the site of the mill lodge (now the park lake) from John Swinglehurst of Park Hill, for the sum of £115.

Abraham married Margaret Whittham at Colne Parish Church on February 11th 1766 and the newlyweds lived, for a while at least, at Heirs House in Colne. In his final two years Abraham suffered from a series of debilitating strokes which finally rendered him paralysed - in the inimitable manner of the day his condition saw him certified as a 'lunatic' shortly before his death in 1804.

The Hargreaves family appear to have carried on running the mill following Abraham's death until it was taken over, possibly by William Eltoft, in 1811. In 1823 it was sold to Thomas Smith of Netherheys for £1,990 and the advance over the price of £233 paid by Abraham in 1783 reflects the massive amount of improvement carried out over the interim period. In 1824 Thomas Smith leased the mill to William Brightmore and John Hudson for 18 years at a price of £231 per annum.

The Old Mill Caul: 1905

Until 1784 the Old Mill caul was a stone structure with timber boards across the top. This arrangement allowed for a head of water in the 'Stannery' at the top of the caul so that water could be diverted via the main sluice gate to the mill. In December 1656 Christopher Towneley, of Carr Hall and Carr Mill, brought two of his estate workers, farmer John Varley and carpenter George Pollard, to Barrowford where they intended to destroy the Barrowford mill caul. A court deposition describes the event:

'Christopher Towneley by force and arms that is to say with staffs clubs and axes and other weapons of offence did use them to mob riotously and did congregate and unlawfully assemble together to the great terror of the people of this Commonwealth with the intent to destroy by force and wantonly one mill caul standing upon a river called Barrowford which was set to supply a certain mill there called Barrowford Mill being in the possession of Christopher T[...] and James Wilson and did break and pull up by reason whereof the aforesaid mill was made useless to the great damage of them the said Christopher T[...] and James Wilson.' - *Towneley's obvious intent was to disable the rival mill in order to gain more business for his own venture.*

When Brightmore and Hudson took over the mill in 1824 they were allowed to; *'Install an engine house and to put in an engine worked by steam'* and this meant that the mill was probably being partially powered by steam almost ten years before the Higherford Mill installed their own engine. In 1839 the lease of the Old Mill was transferred to Henry Armistead and John Tunstill (whose partnership was dissolved in 1842 – Armistead going bankrupt in 1848) and by 1865 Jonathan Stansfield (builder of the Blacko Tower) had taken the lease for 5 years at an annual rent of 100 guineas.

Jonathan Stansfield went bankrupt in 1873 and the lease went to Stephen ('Stivvy') Stow (1835-1885) and partners, the last partner being John Fell who withdrew in 1882, Stephen carrying on until his death in 1885. Before taking over the mill Stephen had kept Spring Lane Farm at Colne and his great granddaughter, Dorothy Turner (née Stow) recalls family stories of him buying cattle in Scotland and driving them down to Colne before returning them when they were fattened and ready for sale. At that time droving could be a dangerous occupation on account of the many bandits who operated along the routes, waiting for a drover on his return journey when he was likely to be carrying money. Stephen was almost waylaid one day on his return from Scotland; his horse suddenly leaped into the air as they were trotting along a dirt road. Looking back to see why the horse had behaved so erratically Stephen noticed that it had jumped over a taught length of wire stretched from tree to tree across the lane – the purpose of which had been to bring down the horse and rider in order to rob him.

Stephen and Sarah Stow: c.1880

Old Mill Cottages: c.1880

From a painting by a travelling artist
This picture, and the portraits of Stephen and Sarah Stow, kindly supplied by Dorothy and Simon Turner

Stephen Stow married a Colne girl, Sarah Briggs (1837-1907) and had 7 children, one of whom died in infancy. When running the mill the family lived in the Mill Cottage situated on the river bank close to the mill buildings.

This picture of the cottages shows the outlet of the bypass sluice (the square opening on the water's edge). This took the form of a culvert running from the 'live' side of the water wheel along which water could be directed beneath the cottages and into the river when not required to drive the wheel. In particularly bad weather it was necessary for the bypass sluice to be opened to prevent an unwanted build-up of water within the leats and the lodge and Stephen Stow's children remembered the roar of the water beneath their cottage when their father had need to release it in the middle of stormy nights. The culvert opening is walled up now but it can still be made out with a little detective work.

The cottages were erected during the eighteenth century, probably by Abraham Hargreaves, to house the mill overlookers whose presence on site meant that they could monitor the mill 24 hours per day. In 1841 the resident overlooker at the mill cottages was Thomas Shuttleworth (25) who lived there with his wife Margaret (25) and son James (3) – the other mill cottage being unoccupied at that time. Attached to the mill were a further 7 cottages across the river in the Old Row area.

Following Stephen Stow's death in 1885 his widow, Sarah, continued to run the Old Mill for a further two years and her departure in 1887 saw the end of the mill as a spinning operation (almost exactly one-hundred years after its inception by Abraham Hargreaves). The Stow family went to live at Auburn House on Halstead Lane where they stayed for a number of years - here the family were well known for their expertise in breeding championship standard racing pigeons.

Stephen Stow and Family: 1927

This photograph shows another 'Stivvy' Stow who was a member of a branch of the Stow family. He lived on Corlass Street with his wife, Carrie, and bred racing pigeons. He is shown here on his allotment on Bull Holme. L to R: Rosie Birch of 6 Victoria Street – Stivvy Stow holding Rosie's son, Frank –Carrie Stow – Carrie's niece

Two of Stephen and Sarah Stow's sons formed their own weaving concern in 1908 and took space at Sam Holden's new Holmefield Mills at Newbridge. At this time Sam Holden leased room and power at his mill to a number of small manufacturers until he took all the space for his own company in 1930. The Stow brothers were the last of the tenants to leave Holmefield from where they moved to Hindley in 1930.

The Old Mill was used by a number of trades after its demise as a spinning mill; it saw life as a leather works, dye works and motor cycle repair shop before being purchased by the council in 1924 – the inevitable demolition and clearance of the ancient site followed in 1932.

Looking Across the Site of Barrowford Park

The old Vicarage can be seen to the left with Oaklands House behind and Albert Mills to the right

John Dixon was a manufacturer at Lower Clough Mill, Walverden Shed and Holmefield Mill and it is thanks to his foresight and generosity that Barrowford has been able to enjoy the park that has played an integral part within the village for over eighty years. On 18th May 1922 John Dixon donated the land for Barrowford Park (the land known as *Mill Holme* and *Coney Garth*) to the Urban District Council. On the same day Samuel Holden, owner of the Holmefield Mills, gave the Bull Holme for the creation of the recreation ground. Together at 15 acres the lands were bought by Holden and Dixon when land at Lower Park Hill Farm came up for sale. The purchase price was £3,125 and a further 17 acres were purchased by public subscription at a cost of £1,325. Work commenced and the mill leat from the lodge to the old mill was filled in and made into a footpath in June 1925.

Left: John Dixon
Right: Sam Holden

Coney Garth

The high ridge forming the backdrop to the park is almost certainly the feature from which Barrowford derives its name. The Old English (Anglo-Saxon) word *béaru* denotes a wooded embankment and the *ford* suffix relates to the old river crossing across from where the Fleece Inn stood.

Towards the Park Hill end of the ridge are two distinct hollows carved out of the hill. These were partly formed by the action of the river but the hand of man played a part when marl was extracted from the banking. Marl is a type of sandy gravel used extensively for feeding and improving the soil. When the local land first began to be taken into agricultural production, over a period ranging from the thirteenth to sixteenth centuries, marl was quarried from a number of *'penny pits'* within the extended district and the material was spread on the land. This allowed for a breaking up of the clayey soil and the nutrients in the gravel helped to increase the fertility of the land for growing crops (including grass).

Coney Garth forms one of these hollow features along with the one in which the Park Hill complex sits. This latter hollow was known as *Ell Hole* where the Old English word *ell* describes a spring that runs down from Tenter Croft and through the Park Hill grounds - *hole* is simply a Saxon word for *hollow*.

Church Street
Taken from an unusual angle this photograph shows houses on Church Street with Blacko Hill in the background.

Before the erection of St. Thomas' Church (in the late 1830s) Church Street was known as Back Lane and this was the main route from Padiham and the Wheatley Lane district through to Colne. The lane ran to Bank Hall before descending down Little Hill to the old ford from where it crossed Mill Holme (now the park) on its way through to Colne.

The top of the brow, where the former Primitive Methodist Chapel stands, was called Bank Stile after the pathway that ran up the side of the original chapel and, through the Long Fields to Lower Fulshaw and over to Roughlee – this path was retained when the first chapel was erected and became known as Barrow Passage. This area saw a number of houses and shops spring up from the end of the eighteenth century and it is fair to say that it was somewhat more select than the neighbouring development around the Old Row. A surprising number of residents within Bank Stile owned several properties here and it was only the restriction of the narrow roadway of Back Lane that prevented the area from being developed to the extent that we see in Newbridge towards the end of the nineteenth century.

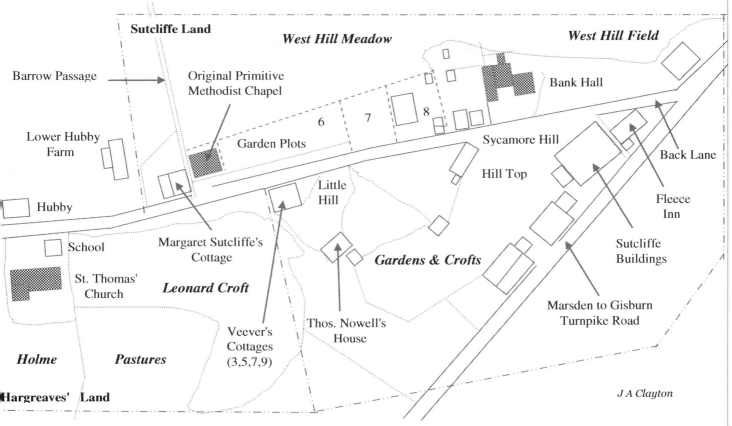

The Bank Stile Area: c. 1845

Sutcliffe Land

West Hill Meadow

West Hill Field

Barrow Passage

Original Primitive
Methodist Chapel

Bank Hall

Lower Hubby
Farm

Garden Plots

6   7   8

Sycamore Hill

Back Lane

Hubby

Hill Top

Fleece
Inn

Little
Hill

Margaret Sutcliffe's
Cottage

School

Gardens & Crofts

Sutcliffe
Buildings

St. Thomas'
Church

Leonard Croft

Veever's
Cottages
(3,5,7,9)

Thos. Nowell's
House

Marsden to Gisburn
Turnpike Road

Holme   *Pastures*

Hargreaves' Land

J A Clayton

John Veever's Cottage (7 and 9 Church Street)

In 1823 the Barrowford Primitive Methodist movement was added to the Sunday Circuit but it did not take hold until 1834 when a room was taken in John Veever's house on the Little Hill area of Bank Stile. This was the first Primitive Methodist indoor meeting room and within 6 months land had been purchased across the road in order to build a new chapel. The land in this area was owned by the Sutcliffe family of Bank Hall and the Hargreaves family of Laund.

The First Primitive Methodist Chapel

In 1834 Margaret Sutcliffe occupied a weaver's cottage fronting on to Church Street, the surrounding area being used as gardens by various local people. Immediately to the west of Margaret's cottage was a croft owned by Thomas Sutcliffe who sold this land in 1834 to Thomas Veevers, a relative of John Veevers. In the following year the foundation stone was laid on this croft site for the new chapel building which opened in 1837 at a cost of £256.

The 'New' Primitive Methodist Chapel

An ancient footpath (the Bank Stile) ran through the croft and it was stipulated that this should be retained at a width of 4 feet, or enough to allow the free passage of a hand-barrow – hence the name Barrow Passage became attached to the extant path. To the east of the croft were *'gardens with all singular houses and outhouses etc.,'* occupied by Emmott Sutcliffe, Thomas Grimshaw and James Walton. These were the first houses to be erected on this side of Church Street (28-36) and were fronted by what became Garden Street.

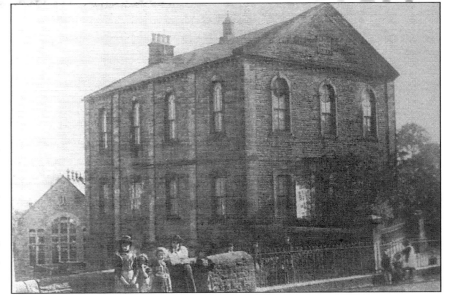

By 1870 the congregation had outgrown the first chapel and in this year land was purchased across the road from James Howarth Hargreaves and in 1871 the foundation stone for a new, larger building was laid by William Tunstill of Reedyford House. The congregation pulled together in the building of the new chapel, as they had done with its predecessor, but unfortunately they did not lay the foundations soundly enough and the new chapel almost fell down before it was half built. The builders started again and, with this extra cost, they almost bankrupted themselves – the final cost being £2,880. However, the strong leadership of the permanent minister, Rev. J S White, saw the debt gradually diminish until it was finally cleared in 1895.

In 1873 the old chapel was sold off to local grocer, Bulcock Duckworth, for the sum of £140 and by 1881 the building had been divided into 4 separate dwellings – it is now 2 houses. Also in 1873 the trustees of the new chapel purchased a garden area in the vicinity of the building.

Site of the Bank Stile

The Bank Stile was the stile in the footpath to Roughlee and was set into the northern boundary of Sutcliffe's West Hill land. In February 1860 William Nutter, a butcher who worked in the family shop on Gisburn Road, was asked by John Barrowclough to skin a horse that had died in the Long Field. William took his whittle (butcher's knife) and set off up the Barrow Passage but when he came to the stile he slipped and the knife sliced through his windpipe, opening the main artery in his neck. The unfortunate man turned back down the passage but immediately collapsed and died from a massive loss of blood.

The cottages comprising numbers 3, 5, 7 and 9 Church Street (of which John Veevers owned number 7 and 9) were later occupied by James Walton who surrendered them in 1872 to Moses Nowell, a mill overlooker. This family farmed the nearby Lower Hubby Causeway Farm and lived in a house that would become the site of the Congregational Chapel. Numbers 7 and 9 were occupied as 2 cottages by William Greenwood and David Dugdale and then, by 1879, Joseph Beesley occupied them as a single dwelling.

In 1880 all of these cottage properties were sold to Rev. Gough, the Congregationalist minister of Halstead Lane – this gave him the option of demolishing the cottages and replacing them with the new chapel that was planned. In the end the new chapel was erected on the site of the Nowell's house while the properties of numbers 1, 3, 5 and 9a, with land adjoining, were sold in 1923 to Samuel Haworth, a retired grocer, for the sum of £450. In 1892 numbers 7 and 9 were purchased by William Roberts, of 33 Church Street, for £130 – all these cottages were demolished in July 1961.

Bank Stile Miscellany (from original deeds):

Ellis Fell sold number 24 Church Street to James Turner (date unclear). This property was owned by Miles Veevers and John Birtwistle and was surrendered by them in 1857 and again changed hands in 1880.

1848: Thomas Veevers erected a joiners shop near to the old Methodist Chapel.

1859: Executors of Thomas Veevers sell to John Veevers for £75 *'all that cottage erected on the close called the 'garden' with yard of 26 yards at the back occupied jointly with cottages adjacent at the back belonging to William Greenwood (plot 7) near the Primitive Methodist Chapel.'*

Deed description: *'Numbers 20, 26 and all those 4 dwellings then in the course of erection (1857) by James Turner, and the right of way along Garden Street laid out on the former 'garden' croft. And a continuation of Garden Street along the front of the Primitive Methodist Chapel adjoining lot 8 and along the front of the cottages belonging to Thomas Nowell, next and adjacent to the PM Chapel, and from the highway called Wheatley Lane. And a right of way for 'foot passengers and wheelbarrows only' along a passage 4-feet wide called Barrow Passage from Garden Street to the northern boundary of plot 6, then along the northerly end of lot 6 into the plot of ground at lot 5.'*

'Numbers 28 and 30 surrendered in 1857 by John Birtwistle of Wall Green, Padiham, farmer, and Miles Veevers of Bury, wheelwright , for £24:10s:0d to James Hartley, labourer, of Barrowford - all that plot of building land called the 'garden' formerly occupied by James Robinson fronting the highway of Wheatley Lane being lot 6. And the right of way over Garden Street recently laid out over 3 plots (lots 6, 7, 8) all part of the 'garden.' In 1853 the land behind 28 and 30, at 101 square yards, was purchased by Hartley Duckworth and Edmund Butterfield. Hartley Duckworth was the son of Bulcock Duckworth who owned 10 Duckworth Street, 38 and 40 Church Street and 38 and 40 Back Church Street.

36 to 20 Church Street (left to right)

1879: The land was formerly conveyed to the Eccles Committee for the site of a parsonage and garden for the incumbent of St. Thomas' Church and an additional plot, part of West Hill Field, was added to the parsonage in 1892. This is now known as the Old Vicarage.

1905: James Hargreaves owned the land upon which the Barrowford Urban District Council town yard was built (Ingham Street); he also owned land at the back of the new Primitive Methodist Chapel and the land between the Council School and Church Street.

We have already met with the cottages on Hill Top but deeds survive for other properties in the wider area of Sycamore Hill within which Hill Top fell. In 1883 numbers 12 and 18 Hill Top were sold by John Brown (a brewer at Clough Springs Brewery) to William Buckle. In 1877 number 10 was sold by James Haworth, of Wheatley Lane, to William Buckle - this property was above the shop at 111 Gisburn Road. James Dugdale (died 1893) owned the land which was eventually sold to the Co-Op. In 1893 Sarah Hargreaves, a spinster of Laund, sold number 17 Hill Top to Betsy Midgeley of the White Bear for £94. She also purchased 19 Hill Top from John W Buckle, grocer, for £60 and numbers 11, 13 and 15 from James Hargreaves of Altrincham, Cheshire, for £255 in 1895. These cottages were the inheritance of James Hargreaves, of Laund and were occupied in 1891 by Margaret Costello, James Buckle and James Jackson Smith.

Looking over the Bowling Green to Hill Top and West Hill Meadow

In 1920 John Brown sold numbers 5, 7 and 9 Hill Top, with a communal garden fronting onto Church Street, to Mr. R Petty of Nelson for £465 - however, these were confusingly referred to in the sale as 3, 5 and 7 Church Street.

Numbers 20 and 22 Church Street, and 115 Gisburn Road, were demolished by the UDC in 1933, the Co-op had sold to the Council part of their land and this became the rose-garden behind the bus-bay on Gisburn Road. In 1877 number 10 Hill Top comprised 2 houses fronting the highway near the Fleece Inn, this was formerly 4 houses. In 1922 John England, painter and decorator of Scotland Rd, Nelson, bought this property, and others, shown as: *'house and shop at 109 Gisburn Road in the occupation of Betsy Buckle, a lock-up shop at 111 Gisburn Road, the dwelling of Harold Dixon (grocer), and the house above number 111 i.e., number 10 Hill Top.'*

1898: All those 5 houses near the Fleece Inn, after the end of the barn, were in the ownership of William Buckle. He left them to Dick Buckle, who still owned them in 1911. In 1922 they were sold to John England

who resold them to the UDC under a clearance order in 1937. A sale notice of 1920 shows *'11-19 Hill Top with vacant land at the rear abutting Church Street.'*

Bank Hall

Now the Lamb Club, Bank Hall started life as a farm house to which Thomas and Grace Sutcliffe (née Hartley) added the porch and wing to gentrify the house in 1696. The land belonging to Bank Hall Farm extended northwards up the hill - south to the river - on either side of Church Street and past the White Bear.

In 1757 Thomas Sutcliffe 'the younger' farmed Bank Hall and in 1769 the occupier was Oddie Sutcliffe 'the elder.' In 1803 Oddie Sutcliffe the elder surrendered to his son, Oddie: *'All that east-end of the messuage and tenement with the east-end of the barn and other buildings: and also the lands adjacent known as The Lastidge - Lastidge Meadow - Higher Rushyfield (and the lane adjacent) - Lower Rushy Field - Orchard - Garden and the backside of the house to the north-west corner opposite.'* This did not relate to Bank Hall but to Lower Ridge Farm situated on the heights above the top of Halstead Lane. The farm was divided into two and Oddie junior was inheriting part of it – by 1841 Oddie's nephew, Thomas Garnett (30), and his family were farming this part of Ridge Farm while a man named Dyson farmed the other.

The lands mentioned in the surrender refer to an area lying between Halsteads Farm and Lower Ridge Farm to the east of the lane connecting the two. The estate plan shows that Halstead Lane was then known as Occupation Lane up the hill to Halsteads Farm after which it became Oddie Gate which signifies *'the road to Oddie's farm.'* The field name of *Lastidge* is interesting in that this is a Scandinavian (Danish) term meaning *'difficult'* thus suggesting that this land was not easy to cultivate and that it might have been occupied at a time either before, or shortly after the Norman invasion of 1066.

Mathew Cragg

The Sutcliffes of Bank Hall also owned a great deal of the land and property at the bottom of Halstead Lane on the site of what was Charles Farm. In 1841 Emmott Sutcliffe (co-owner of Bogmoriles Mill) was farming from here and the barn for this small farm stood at what is now the entrance to Halstead Lane – this was known as Oddie's Barn as late as the 1930s.

Thomas Sutcliffe, who rebuilt Bank House with his wife Grace, died in 1730 leaving a son Thomas and grandson Thomas, who was the father of the above Oddie Sutcliffe 'the elder' (1743-1827). At this time Oddie's son, Oddie Sutcliffe 'the younger,' was a farmer of Bank Hall with his sister Peggy and Edward Cragg (the grandson of his sister Susan and her husband, Mathew Cragg of Salterforth). Oddie the younger died a bachelor in 1857 aged 80. The occupants of Bank Hall in 1861 were Mathew Cragg, widower aged 52, son of Susan Sutcliffe and Mathew Cragg and the father of George and Edward Cragg.

Oddie the younger was the brother of Margaret Sutcliffe who owned the cottages to the west of the old Primitive Methodist Chapel and on her death Oddie inherited these cottages along with the 4 other cottages, the house and garden occupied by Doctor Dickinson (who was living at Bank Hall) and the 18 acre farm. Oddie's will, dated 1851, named 3 nephews, Stephen, Sutcliffe and Thomas Garnett (this latter was farming the Sutcliffe farm of Lower Ridge in 1841) and he left a life interest in all his property to Mathew Cragg. Oddie's 7 cottages and Bank Hall went to Edward Hutchinson Cragg (Mathew's son) for his life and then to his children. The farm went to another of Mathew's sons, George Sutcliffe Cragg. Witnesses to the will were James Harrison, William Corbridge and James Sutcliffe of Water Meetings Farm. Edward Hutchinson Cragg, born in 1834, was an organ builder and died in London in 1910. In 1898 he had sold Bank Hall to John Strickland, a brewer who, as we have seen, sold the property in 1904 to Edmondson Widdup, John Whipp and John Gabbattt of the Working Men's Institute - the Hall then became the Lamb Club as it still remains.

Blocked Doorway

Original Ground Level

Bank Hall – West End

A blocked doorway high in the west gable wall once exited at ground level and this, along with the jettied line of the original foundations, illustrates that the Hall occupied a pronounced mound which has now been reduced to form a new access. The grounds attached to the Hall originally extended back into the West Hill Field and forward all the way down to the riverside where a lime kiln and a smithy operated as part of the Bank Hall farm economy

Bank Farm?

This building stands at the modern entrance to Bank Hall and appears to have been altered beyond recognition – however, there is a likelihood that this property is one of the earliest surviving buildings in Barrowford. Close inspection of the structure reveals that the two corners of the wall alongside the entrance to Bank Hall are original. The unusually large quoin stones in the corners of this gable, and the style of the blocked doorway on the gable, suggest a date of not later than the mid-eighteenth century. It is apparent that the gable was the original frontage of the building and the large former doorway suggests that it was not intended for purely domestic use or, alternatively, it was a building of a status that belies its present size.

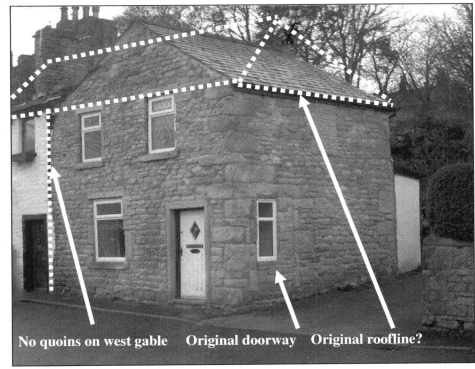

No quoins on west gable   Original doorway   Original roofline?

The present frontage of the door and three windows would originally have been a side wall without reveals and this would probably have stretched back over the area now occupied by the cottage which shares a common wall. This extended building could, then, have been the original barn and mistal. The building line to the rear of the property shows that the back wall of the smaller cottage, being of rubble construction, is different to the build within the end property as is the flush frontage onto Church Street.

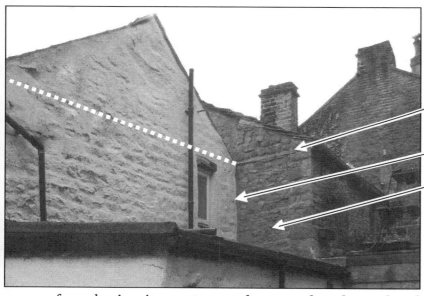

Bank Farm? - Rear Aspect

Original cross-beam level of 1st floor ceiling (roofline *possibly* extended over end property)

No quoins on west gable

Coursed rubble wall infill is not keyed to back wall and suggests a blocked opening

We have, then two adjoined buildings of differing date. The masonry of the gabled building suggests that it is older than its neighbour but, at some stage, it has suffered from having its western end removed to be replaced by a cottage. This suggests a transition from agricultural use to domestic use and is most likely to have occurred after the erection, or upgrade of Bank Hall. At this period the Hall was intended as a high status home for the Sutcliffe family whose farming operations were now concentrated in other parts of the village.

This is not to say that the gable building was half-demolished and provided with an adjoining cottage at the same time that the hall was upgraded in 1696. There is every chance that this building was originally either a laithe-house (with attached barn), a single barn incorporating a mistral or the original dwelling occupied by the farmers at Bank Farm. In the case of the latter the building would predate the new Hall of 1696 and this would put it into the category of a late 16th century to mid-seventeenth century building. Whatever the case may be it is clear that this unassuming building has many secrets to reveal and the Bank Hall site is more than worthy of a properly structured assessment.

St. Thomas' Church: pre-1904

In January 1909 Mr. F O Stanford (C of E) inspected the churchyard and gave permission for it to be extended. In 1911 a plot was taken from The Pastures and the graves extreme right of picture were removed to allow for the formation of a footpath. This photograph is taken from a postcard sent in February 1904 by the St. Thomas' minister, Rev. A F S Studdy. His message on the card reads: *'Sorry there is no better view of the Church to send, but this is the only one to be got, I think. We do not like it, the perspective is too violent.'*

In the early part of the 1830s James Howarth Hargreaves, who owned the land upon which the old St. Thomas' Church School stands, persuaded James Nowell Farrington, of Leyland (who owned the neighbouring land) that if he (Farrington) were to donate land for the erection of a church he (Hargreaves) would match the donation by providing land for a church school. The land for the church was duly donated and the foundation stone was laid by Mrs. Every-Clayton of Carr Hall on the 21st December 1837. A subscription of £750 was raised by the Chester Diocesan Society, alongside local parishes, and the contract for the building work was awarded to the Ducketts of Burnley, one of whom, James Duckett, would go on to found the highly successful Burnley firm of James Duckett Sanitary Ware Manufacturers. Fanny Nowell, the sister of Sarah Nowell who was murdered by her husband in Dixon Street in 1897, was the domestic help for the Duckett family at their home in Accrington Road, Burnley. Fanny had moved north from Staffordshire to find work

at the age of 14 and was happy with the Duckett family. In 1888 the family moved to a new house on Padiham Road and Fanny attended her sister's wedding at St. Thomas' Church earlier in the year. Tragically, by the late autumn Fanny had contracted typhoid fever and died on the 26th October aged 24 years.

The Old Church School and House

The new church building was opened in 1841, enlarged in 1855 and again in 1883 when the chancel was added, the church re-seated and the organ enlarged at the expense of Thomas Barrowclough of Oaklands. The cost of £3,000 for this extension was further to Barrowclough's donation of the church font in 1870.

True to his word James Hargreaves started the ball rolling for a new school by providing abstract of title to his lands in 1849 where he proved that he owned the land of Old Leonard Meadow (sometimes given as Little Leonard Meadow or Leonard Croft) which formed a small part of the large field known as Pastures. An agreement was made that Hargreaves, who had owned the land since 1778, would sell it to the promoters of a National Board School. On the 2nd of April 1851 a Deed of Enfranchisement between Hargreaves and the purchasers was drawn up stating that:

'Part of a close of meadow land formerly called the Pasture Head but lately known as Old Leonard Meadow, bounded in part by a lately existing school house and yard, is to be granted upon trust to be

used for a school and that I James Haworth Hargreaves do grant and assure said premises to the ministers and churchwardens and the premises shall be at all times had and enjoyed upon trust without let or hindrance of me or any of my descendants or ancestors.'

Witnesses to the deed were James H Hargreaves, the Steward of the Forest of Pendle, Samuel Smith (minister), John Barrowclough (churchwarden) and John Ingham (churchwarden). A School Management Committee was set up to run the school and this consisted of the principal officiating minister, his licensed curate and three other persons resident within the parish – these latter three were elected on the highest number of votes obtained from contributors who paid ten shillings for each vote (up to a maximum of 6 votes). All members, contributors, teachers and mistresses were to be members of the United Church of England and Ireland and the officiating minister of Barrowford parish was to serve as Chairman of the Committee. A Ladies Committee of not more than six ladies was set up to oversee good practice in the education of the infants and girls

St. Thomas' School Group 2: 1904 My grandfather is 6th from the left on the back row

By 1921 the system of contributors paying for the privilege of voting for the Committee members was breaking down and, furthermore, new laws had changed the way in which church schools were to be run. In 1902 the Education Act stated that each school should have 6 Managers, 2 of whom would be appointed directly by the Local Education Committee. However, after much bluster and wasted time an Act of 1904 stated that the managers of Barrowford Church School would be subject to exactly the same constraints as they had been within the original Deed of Enfranchisement in 1851 other than the curates could not serve on the Committee!

A Wedding at St. Thomas' in 1947

In 1921 Rev. F W Fairhurst, of St. Thomas', wrote to the National Society in London for guidance relating to the fact that it had become difficult to find people willing to become contributors. His answer was a somewhat confusing statement that: *'The Minister and Churchwardens are Trustees ex officio, but the Churchwardens are not ex officio Managers.'* Furthermore the National Society suggested that Rev. Fairhurst should gather together new contributors willing to pay 10 shillings per year in order to appoint new school managers regularly.

A provisional school house was erected in 1838 when the church was being built and this was the residence for many of the school teachers - the first official Board teacher, David Smalley, was contracted in 1850 and the first mistress was Mrs. Holden. In 1843 there were 4 'daily' schools, 1 infants school and 1 Sunday school in Barrowford. In December of 1950 the Barrowford Church of England School was officially declared exempt from the Education Act of 1944 as *reverter proviso* – this was due to the fact that Section 2 of the School Sites Act of 1841 did not apply as the school was conveyed to trustees under the authority of the said Section 2 on April 2nd 1851 - the school having been granted by the Duke of Buccleuch (Lord of the Forest of Pendle – through his Steward) and James Haworth Hargreaves.

David Smalley, the first schoolmaster at St. Thomas', was well known for his strict attitude to discipline and would send boys out to cut a hazel switch from the local hedgerows when the need to whack an errant pupil arose. On one occasion Smalley's aptitude with the stick backfired on him when he beat a lad named Gray in front of the whole school for spoiling his copybook. Soon afterwards the unfortunate boy died and Smalley was indicted to appear at the inquest at the Fleece Inn. The jury decided that Smalley should be sent to the Crown Court at Liverpool where a number of local worthies (including the vicar, Rev. Smith) testified for his good character. Eventually the accused was acquitted but it would be interesting to know if his handiness with the cane was thereafter compromised by these unfortunate events.

The Rev. Samuel Smith M.A.
Rector of Barrowford 1842-1877

The first vicar of St. Thomas' was the Rev. Samuel Smith of whom Jesse Blakey, author of the Annals of Barrowford, had the highest opinion. On October 12th 1842 Rev. Smith married Frances Jane Matilda Brooks, third daughter of the late Major Joseph Brooks of Everton, at St. George's, Everton. Before this he had been the curate at Fairford in Gloucestershire and he and his new wife arrived in Barrowford following their marriage.

The Reverend lived with his wife and two spinster sisters at The Grove in Wheatley Lane Road where he was to suffer the loss of his only daughter. His two sisters objected to the schoolchildren of Barrowford wearing curls in their hair and roses in their hats, even on special days such as the annual village rushbearing. Always happy to organise collections for the needy one of Rev. Smith's beneficiaries was the Soldiers' Infants Home, this was the only asylum within the British Empire catering for the daughters of non-commissioned officers and relatives of the army, orphans or not. To this cause he donated, in July 1856, the proceeds of the Vicarage of Barrowford Church Collectors amounting to the sum of £2: 2s: 0d – another £2: 10s :9d was donated in June 1859.

Old St. Thomas' Church: 2009

St. Thomas' could boast a renowned church choir and in 1875 the members were;

Elizabeth Hargreaves; Dinah Bradshaw; Sarah Sutcliffe; Alice Roberts; Elizabeth Foulds; Elizabeth Nutter; Alice Ridehalgh; Susan Lee; Betsy Lee; Isabella Butler; Maggie Butler; Nancy Eastwood; Mary Kendal; Jane Hartley; Daniel Nutter; Richard Holden; Hamlett Nutter; William Skinner; Hartley Skinner; John Kendal; William Hargreaves; Ezra Bolton; Thomas Pickover; Humphrey Howarth; Thomas Nutter.

Assistant curates to Rev. Samuel Smith were;

1844-46; William Holt Duncan
1846-48; Theodore Budd
1848-51; Robert Smyth Weldon
1852-53; William Newsham
1854-56; George Hillyard
1866-67; Robert Cowburn
1867-68; Richard Willdig
1868-69; Thomas Chapman
1870-73; Ricketts Raymond Ricketts
1873-74; Charles Cary Bull
1874-76; John Heyworth Grimshaw
1876-77; Robert Henry Towneley

Organists at the church were;

1843: Abraham Holt built the first organ and was the first organist
2nd was Ormerod Barrowclough
3rd was Mrs. Every Clayton
4th was John Pollard
5th was Henry Bolton
6th was Robert Rushton
7th was Thomas Brooks
8th was Varley Moore
1900: William Mantle was confirmed as the organ blower for 5 years and Humphrey Haworth was the choirmaster.

St. Thomas' Interior: 1940s

The second vicar of St. Thomas' was the Rev. Alfred Freeman Studdy Studdy who came to the parish from Astley, Bolton, in 1877 where he had served for two years. Rev. Studdy stayed at Barrowford until 1913 and he died on the Wirral in 1925. His incumbency was not without the odd controversial event - on Thursday 3rd of November 1881, for instance, a Barrowford man named Edwin Woofinden (31) died at his Barrowford home. It so happened that Mr. Woofinden was Wesleyan Methodist and the only choice for the family at this time was to bury him at either the Wheatley Lane Methodist Chapel or at St. Thomas'. However, as Mr. Woofinden had expressed a wish to be buried at the latter his wife approached Rev. Studdy in order to purchase a well located plot that she had her eye on.

The Woofinden Memorial Stone

Unfortunately for Mrs. Woofinden Rev. Studdy would not allow her to purchase that particular plot if, as she wanted, the burial rites were to be performed by the local Wesleyan minister, Rev. I Fairburn. According to the widow Rev. Studdy told her that if he were not to be allowed to perform the service then she would have to be content with a less favourable burial plot i.e., *'under the area used to tip the church boiler ashes, provided that the ashes were then replaced or she might have a grave for ten shillings but her husband would have to be buried with another body.'*

As a consequence of this Mrs. Woofinden sought advice from the Methodist Church and was advised to take the grave plot that she wanted rather have the services of the minister that she wanted. The interment took place on the following Tuesday, 8th of November. As a protest the Rev. E Gough (Congregationalist) and the Rev. I Fairburn (Wesleyan) went with the funeral party but left it at the church gates. A letter subsequent to this was sent to the Home Secretary and the

National daily press reported the incident as *A burial Scandal*. The letter was written by the secretaries of the Legal Committee appointed by the Wesleyan Methodist Conference and it stated that upon Mr. Woofinden's death legal notice was served upon the Rev. Studdy (of St. Thomas's) that the burial would be conducted by the local Wesleyan minister. Rev. Studdy consented to the plot of ground chosen by the relatives but afterwards, learning that the deceased was a Dissenter, he replied that they could not have the ground they had selected, but that the deceased must be buried where they could find room.

The letter also said that: *'The right claimed by the clergy to exercise an uncontrolled discretion in the appropriation of burial sites in parish church yards may frequently render the Burials Act inoperative. It is hoped that the Home Secretary will take steps to prevent the recurrence of such conduct as at Barrowford.'* The Act referred to here was Section 7 of the Burial Laws Amendment Act of September 1880 under which it is an offence to: *Wilfully endeavour to bring into contempt or obloquy the Christian religion, or the belief or worship of any church or denomination of Christians, or the members or any minister of any such church or denomination.* The Burial Act was amended shortly afterwards (possibly as a result of the Barrowford debacle) to enable burials to take place within churchyards without the rites of the Church of England. Unsurprisingly this state of affairs caused uproar within the village.

One day in 1964 the neighbourhood around St. Thomas' awoke to a strong smell of smoke in the morning air through which could be heard the final, mournful toll of the church bell as it glowed in the heat of the fire that was to destroy the church. The ravaged building was never rebuilt and its forlorn shell now shelters a garden of remembrance.

The New St. Thomas' Church Building of c.1970

Barrowford Board School: c.1905

The first Barrowford School Board was created in December 1874 and the initial meeting took place at the Primitive Methodist Chapel under the chairmanship of Thomas Barrowclough and Rev. Samuel Smith. Dr. Little was the first vice-president, John Fieldhouse the clerk and other members were Hartley Horsfield and Thomas Berry. In 1875 the Reverend E Gough and S Garnett were elected to the Board and Thomas Grimshaw replaced Rev. Smith. Both the outlying areas of Brogden and Admergill came under the auspices of the Barrowford School Board.

In 1905 there were 4 schools in Barrowford – The Barrowford Central Board School (Rushton Street) – The Newbridge Wesleyan Infants School - The Barrowford National Church of England Voluntary School (St. Thomas') and St. Peter and Paul Catholic Junior School in Higherford.

Barrowford Board School
Infants 1902

Hubby Causeway

Almost directly across from the entrance gates to the old St. Thomas' church stood a cottage known as The Hubby (an old word meaning *small roadside farm*). The Hubby gave its name to Hubby Causeway, the stretch of road 8 roods in length running from the top of Bank Stile westward to the beginning of Wheatley Lane Road near Clough Farm.

A name that was synonomous with the Hubby for over fifty years was that of Bolton. John Bolton married Ann Sutcliffe andbetween them they had 20 surviving children, Rushton being the youngest of them. What is now the Oaklands Home Farm was known as Lower Hubby Causeway and living there in 1845 was William Baldwin who owned and occupied the; *'house, garden, barn, mistal, pasture and holme together rated at £42: 7s: 6d.'*

John Brown farmed Trough Laithe Farm alongside his business as a part-time property auctioneer. Brown was responsible for selling many farms around the district during the later nineteenth century, an example being an auction he carried out in September 1857 for the sale of the Lower Hubby Causeway buildings of *a house, garden, barn and mistal in the possession of Thomas Nowell*. Also for sale are all of the surrounding fields around the Hubby on which some of the cottages of Church Street and Back Church Street now stand. Particulars for the auction were to be had from Mr Stephen Wilson's house (the George and Dragon) or from Mr Ingham Walton of Bank House. Robert Hayurst is in possession of the original large poster relating to the sale where it is stated that one of the fields, named Hole Hurst and Holme, would be suitable for the erection of a mansion house. This, however, was not to be and in the early 1950s

the housing estates of Oaklands Avenue and Higher Causeway were built on this land. The fields above the Hubby were called Hubbycourse Meadow and Barn Field – John Barrowclough built his Oaklands House on the boundary between these areas of land. The Hubby was demolished around 1870 to make way for the Oaklands Lodge.

Higher Causeway Barn and House

Opposite to Hubby Causeway, next to the old St. Thomas' churchyard, is to be found a barn conversion once known as Hubby Causeway Barn. This was probably a barn attached to the to the Lower Hubby Farm estate. A plan of 1847 shows that the yard attached to the barn (which is possibly of late 18th century date) occupied the western end where the large Higher Causeway House is now attached.

This higher status house was always known as 'Lonsdale's House' in the earlier part of the 20th century after the family of that name who lived there. At the end of the high walled gardens to the west of Lonsdale's House stands a solitary gatepost which bears testionony to the days when the road here was a dirt track with a gate across. Here, where the new vicarage now stands, was a trackway which branched off Hubby Causeway down to Lower Clough Farm and onward to the ford over the river at Reedyford. This area, where Higher Causeway now meets with Church Street, was known as Grey Stiles, probably as a reference to the age of the path or trackway.

Higher Causeway House(Frontage)

HigherCauseway House appears to have been built in the 1850s on a croft attched to the west side of Causeway Barn. Living at Causeway House in 1861 were Elizabeth Greenwood (65), the head of household and a landed proprietor born in Barrowford. Along with Elizabeth we find her daughter Alice Uttley (35), who had been born in Habergham Eaves, the husband of Alice, Hiram Uttley (49), an assistant surgeon from Heptonstall, a vistitor named Ellen Livesey (34), from Clapham and the housemaid, Mary Carr (15), from Gisburn.

Elizabeth Greenwood died in March 1866 leaving her daughter and son-in-law at Causeway House. By 1871 Uttley (59) had become a qualified surgeon and employed a maid, Elizabeth Hale (28), from Kirkby Stephen. Doctor Uttley went on to build Uttley House which stands on the corner between Ann Street and Uttley Street (where Higher Causeway joins with Gisburn Road).

Also at Causeway House in 1871 were Robinson Duckworth (42), a self-acting winder from Barley, his wife Jane (43), also from Barley, daughters Leah (16), a weaver, Rachel (13), a piecer, Alice (11), a creeler and son John (2). The occupation of each girl is a nice example of the way in which school-leavers progressed through the mill – starting as creelers they would learn each job along the way until they became weavers. Dr. Uttley died in March 1877 and the 1881 census shows his widow, Alice, still at Causeway House where she is living off the income from 'land and railway stocks.' With her is the maid, Elizabeth L.... (28), from Gisburn.

Clough Farm and Clough Springs Brewery: c.1945 Wheatley Springs Barn is just visble extreme left

The Clough Farm estate comprised a number of agricultural buildings along with a 'mansion house.' The farm took its name from Collings Clough which is the deep clough formed by a stream that originates on the ridge near to Higher Fulshaw Farm and runs down to the river at Lower Clough Mill. The name *Collings* is from *coal ings,* an earlier name for the *Coal Pit Field* below Lower Fulshaw through which the Clough stream runs.

Clough is mentioned in the journal of John Wesley who came to preach here in 1774 and 1776. Jesse Blakey relates that the preacher stood in the Clough Farm fold with his back against a tree and his attentive audience gathered on the rising ground in front of him. When some old furniture was removed from Pasture Farm, once the home of Jonas Maud, a bedstead was purchased by a man named John Fielding from Nelson who found hidden within a compartment in the frame a note saying that John Wesley had once slept in the bed.

In the latter part of the eighteenth century the Dent family owned Clough and in 1803 Thomas Robinson farmed its 35 acres. By 1834 Thomas Corlass was living at Clough House (this was a separate property to the farm) – Corlass was in partnership with his brother John as cotton worsted spinning manufacturers. Unfortunately, in 1834 they were declared bankrupt.

Clough Farm (House): c.1945
Looking down Wheatley Lane Road:
St. Thomas' tower in the background

In 1841 Louisa Brightmore (40) was farming at Clough along with her son, William (15), daughter Mary (10) and live-in farm labourer, William Wilson (28). Louisa (a widow) was at that time a part owner of the Barrowford Old Mill, her husband William Brightmore having leased it (with John Hudson) from Thomas Smith for 18 years at £231 per annum. In 1861 Louisa Brightmore (61) was still farming at Clough with her son Thomas (41), daughter Mary (28) and William Wilson (48) who was still the live-in farm labourer.

The 1871 census tells us that Clough Farm had expanded to 38 acres and running the farm were William Sutcliffe (58), born in Marsden (Nelson), his wife Sarah (65), from Foulridge, daughter Helen (12), born in Barrowford and son Hartley (10), also from Barrowford. Keeping up the Wesleyan connection here was a

lodger at the farm in the form of John Aldred (24), the Barrowford Wesleyan minister who originally hailed from Swinton. In 1881 William Sutcliffe (68) was still the farmer emloying two men at Clough although his place of birth was now given as Trawden. Sarah (64) was still there along with son Hartley (24), a farm labourer, Mary King (26), a lodger and a weaver from Foulridge, Mary's sister Ann King (34), also a lodger and a weaver from Foulridge, Mitchell Dewhurst (20), a lodger and farm labourer from Barley and Thomas Berry (17), a lodger and a carter from Kildwick.

Also in 1871 we see that Rev. Samuel Smith (65), vicar of Barrowford (born Epsom in Surrey) was now a widower (his wife Frances Jane having died in 1861) and had moved down the hill from The Grove to live at Clough. Others were Robert Hargreaves (44), a coachman from Grindleton, Ann Hitchen (44), a cook also from Grindleton and Sarah Grace Walton (19), a housemaid from Clitheroe.

Clough Barn rack-stone inclusions

Clough Barn is now called Wheatley Springs Barn; this property is the only remaining building from Clough Farm. The barn incorporates a number of grooved rack stones that once formed the floor of a corn drying kiln. This suggests that there was a kiln in the Clough area before the barn was built (possibly around 1790-1820) and might even be an indication of early brewing on the site. A field called the Kiln Field was attached to Higher Fulshaw Farm and it is worth considering that the kiln that once stood here was quarried for stone to build the Clough Barn

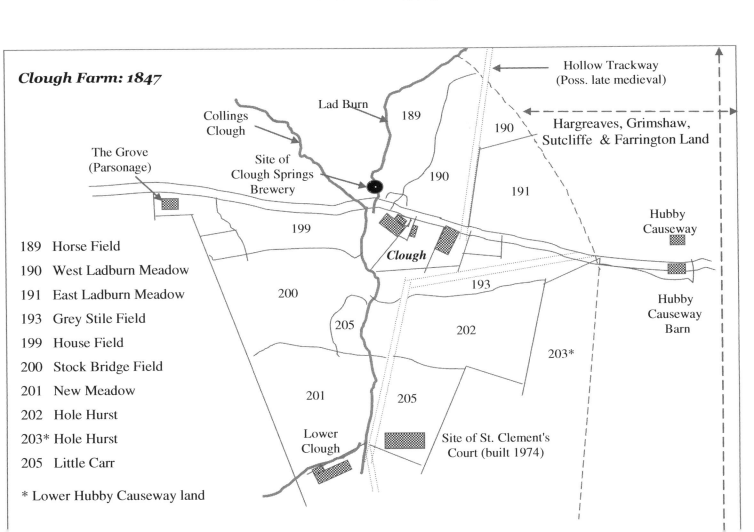

Clough Farm: 1847

The Grove
(Parsonage)

Collings
Clough

Site of
Clough Springs
Brewery

Lad Burn

189

190

190

191

Hollow Trackway
(Poss. late medieval)

Hargreaves, Grimshaw,
Sutcliffe & Farrington Land

Hubby
Causeway

Clough

199

200

205

193

202

203*

Hubby
Causeway
Barn

201

205

Lower
Clough

Site of St. Clement's
Court (built 1974)

189 Horse Field

190 West Ladburn Meadow

191 East Ladburn Meadow

193 Grey Stile Field

199 House Field

200 Stock Bridge Field

201 New Meadow

202 Hole Hurst

203* Hole Hurst

205 Little Carr

* Lower Hubby Causeway land

The Clough House Scene: Then and Now

In 1891 the Clough farm, land, garden, orchard, barn, mistal and stables passed into the ownership of John Holt, of the Park Hill estate and in 1896 Hartley Sutcliffe had taken over the Clough tenancy from his father. Following the death of John Holt and his wife Anne in 1920 the farm was purchased by James Ridehalgh who died in 1936; the executors of his estate then leased the Clough Farm complex to Arthur Lawson Dean who also leased the Clough Springs Brewery buildings (across the road from Clough) from where he operated his Nelson Corn Mills. By 1846 James Hayhurst was the tenant at Clough. Clough Farm was transferred from Arthur Dean to Barrowford Council in 1951 and the farm subsequently stood empty. At this time the Clough land was farmed by the Begley family of Oaklands Home Farm (formerly Lower Hubby Causeway Farm) and was commonly known to the locals as Begley's Fields. The Wheatley Springs estate now occupies the site.

Clough Springs Brewery

The top floor of the 19th century brewing tower was added after 1938

Almost directly opposite to Clough Farm stood the Clough Springs Brewery - this was sited, for obvious reasons, upon a reliable source of water. The brewery was built over a stream that was known centuries ago as Lad Burn (the Old English *Lad = hill* and *burn = stream)* and close to another stream, Collings Clough, which gave the area its name. A tunnel beneath the brewery connected to this latter stream and this formed the original outlet, or waste water drain. John Hartley, who owned a brewery in Colne, founded the brewing operation at Clough around 1852 and, by 1861, he was employing 4 men - this suggests that the business was still in a fledgeling state.

The 1861 census returns for the Clough Brewery lists John Hartley (35), a brewer employing 4 men and born in Marsden. His wife, Ann (38) was from Ripponden, daughter Margaret (6), from Barrowford, son James (3), from Barrowford and daughter Mary (11 months) was also born in Barrowford. Living in a small cottage, apparantly at Clough Brewery, were Thomas Chapman (22), a scripture reader from Astley and his wife Elizabeth (no age recorded) from Astley. John Hartley died in 1867 and the brewery was taken over by the partnership of Thompson and Wignall and then by Thomas Thompson alone.

In 1871 the occupants at the Clough Brewery were Thomas Thompson (47), a master brewer from Skipton employing 6 men. Living with Thomas were his son John (19), a book keeper born in Skipton, daughter Mary (17), no occupation, from Skipton, Son James (12), a scholar from Skpton, son Marten (9), also a scholar from Skipton, son Harry (4), from Nelson and daughter Lily (6), from Skipton. Thomas Thompson's sister, Harriet Brotherton (49), a dressmaker from Skipton, was a visitor along with her daughter Lily Brotherton (14), a general servant from Manchester, and Isabell Robinson (27), with no occupation, from Skipton. Living in the Clough Springs cottage we find Lazarus Pickles (35), from Colne, who was the night watchman at the brewery, and his wife Margaret (35), a weaver from Bacup.

By 1875 John Hartley's son, Robert Hartley, had acquired the business which he ran with his partner, Alexander Bell. On the 11th March 1876 Robert Hartley appeared at Manchester Assizes where he was being sued for damages. The case revolved around Hartley's courtship of the daughter of William Wignall of Ingleton. Wignall was the former partner of Thomas Thompson at Clough Springs and, by the time of the court case, was described as a baker. It was stated in court that Hartley had seduced Wignall's daughter under the promise of marriage but, getting cold feet, he reneged on his promise. Wignall sued for damages and was awarded the not inconsiderable sum of £500.

This was not to be the end of Robert Hartley's woes as things were to become a whole lot worse for the brewer. On Monday the 7th November 1887 he was found collapsed on the pavement opposite his Colne home with blood pouring from a large wound to his head. Unfortunately Hartley died from his wounds on the following day and the police launched a murder enquiry but eventually decided that there had been no foul play involved - no satisfactory explanation for Hartley's wounds was ever provided. Following his partner's untimely demise Alexander Bell left the brewery and became a cotton manufacturer at Fir Trees in Higham.

By 1881 the brewer at Clough Springs was the aptly named Jonas Brewer (60), from Earby. His wife Lucy (30), was a dressmaker from Barrowford and with the couple were their children who had all been born in Barrowford; Arthur (18), an apprentice joiner, James (16), an apprentice cooper at the brewery, Albert (14), an apprentice tin plate worker, Jane (12), a scholar and John (8). Workers at the brewery in 1881 included John Lund (34), a labourer who lived on the main road, John Bowker (35), a labourer from Grassington, Chippendale Walton (65), of Higherford was the warehouseman, John Haselwood (37), originally from Malton but now living on Calder Vale, was the brewery salesman, John Silverwood (36), lived in one of the Club Houses and was a carter and the accountant at the firm was James Jackson (41) who lived on Gisburn Road.

Following Hartley and Bell into Clough Springs was John Kenyon who lived in a house called 'Brymbella' in Rawtenstall and owned the Rossendale Brewery. Kenyon enlarged Clough Springs and in 1890 there was a near fatality when a full barrel of beer rolled onto brewer Jonas Brown – although he suffered a smashed collarbone Brown was able to continue with his work. In 1906 John Kenyon's key employees were Mr. Birchall, the travelling salesman, Mr. Barnes, the book keeper, Jonas Brown, the brewer and Arthur Brown, the assistant brewer – the telephone number for the firm at this time was 46. Kenyon also owned a number of public houses which were tied to his brewing operations, one of these being the Black Bull Inn on Market Street, Colne. The Bridge Inn at Barrowford was also a Hartley and Bells tied house and until recently had a front window that was engraved with *'Hartley and Bells Noted Ales, Barrowford.'*

Masseys Burnley Brewery took over from John Kenyon Limited in 1921 but did not brew on the Clough site, eventually the buildings were partly occupied by Arthur L Dean's operation of the Nelson Corn Mills Limited. In 1949-50 Burnley Club Breweries of Keighley Green reintroduced beer brewing and later the operation took the name of the Lancashire Clubs Brewery Limited which went into liquidation in 1960. The Nelson Corn Mills still continued to occupy buildings to the rear of the main brewery and they also had an egg-grading department in the old malt kiln at Higherford. In 1938 the delivery drivers for the Corn Mills were K Lund, Fred Driver, Fred Stansfield, Jeffrey West (who also ran the Laund Cafe at the top of Wheatley Lane Road) and Harry Hugget. The Corn Mills left the Clough site in 1962 and the brewery began to brew beer once more when Gibbs Keg Brewery Ltd. (Gibbs Mew of Salisbury) upgraded the plant and extended the workforce to around 60. This was not a success, however, and the company left in the late 1960s – their chain of public houses was eventually swallowed up by Enterprise Inns in 1998 and the onle beer now brewed in their name is made at Witney by Refresh Uk.

The Clough Springs site was taken over by Hammonds Sauce after Gibbs had left and they employed the beer brewing equipment, some of it dating back into the nineteenth century, to brew their brand of malt vinegar. I have fond memories of working at the vinegar works in the early 1970s, even though we started the day at 5.30am! The vinegar brewing operation was little different to that of beer brewing; on the day before a brew the sacks of flaked corn were wheeled from the upper floor of the warehouse to the third floor of the tower where they were emptied into the hopper of a crushing machine. The crushed corn, along with malted grain, then collected in a massive hopper on the floor below ready to be used in the brew.

At 5.30am on the next day two of us 'knocked down' the large quantity of grain from the funnel-shaped hopper with long wooden poles; the skill here was to provide a continuous and even flow of grain into the great copper mash tun on the floor below. When the last of the grain had emptied into the tun it formed an even layer of about two feet in depth and a type of rotating sprinkler arm then sprayed hot water over it. The wet grain was the *mash* and the sweet-smelling dark liquor that drained from the tun was the *wort*. This liquor was collected in huge plastic vats that were suspended between two floors and, when buckets of spent brewer's yeast from Masseys Burnley Brewery was added the fermentation process began. The smell from the fermenting vats was something to behold and brought back vivid memories of childhood when we played in the Rushton Street Junior School yard and the sweet, malty aroma of the Lancashire Clubs newly brewed ale would drift down the hill and almost knock us off our feet! Following the initial fermentation process the liquid was piped to the back of the brewery where a series of tall storage vats held it until it had turned into malt vinegar and was ready to be collected by the Hammonds tankers for its journey to their Yorkshire bottling plant.

I recall an incident in 1972 when one of the lads operating a fork lift truck on the ground floor forgot to lower the arms of the vehicle. The problem on this floor level was that the bottom of the massive plastic vats protruded down to almost head-height and below this were the sumps for the outlet pipes. As the fork lift swung around it knocked off one of the sumps and all hell was let loose. We were almost swilled out of the building by the resultant flow of tens of thousands of gallons of semi-brewed acidic liquor. Unfortunately there was nowhere for the liquid to go except into the surface water sewer. Now, yeast and sewage systems are not the ideal bedfellows as the yeast upsets the fine balance of bacteria in the sewage filter beds. Within a short period of the spillage an irate man from the Water Board rang the brewery to say that the sewage works, and the surrounding area, had disappeared beneath a deep blanket of yellow foam and did we know anything about it?

Hammonds carried on their operations at Clough Springs until the 1990s when a series of other companies took over, the last one being Uniqfoods, of Littleborough near Rochdale, who arrived in 1999. The brewery tower in particular, complete as it was with all the necessary brewing equipment, was worthy of preservation as an excellent example of nineteenth century brewing practice. However, when Uniqfoods ceased production at the site in the summer of 2000 (with the loss of 16 jobs) the writing was on the wall for Clough Springs and the site went the way of most of Barrowford's industrial heritage - the old brewery complex was demolished in 2002 to make way for a large apartment block.

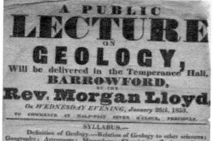

Publicity Poster – Temperance Hall: 1853

To finish this tour of central Barrowford we head back up the village to the eastern limit set for the subject area of this book and that is Pasture Lane. Climbing up the Lane from Bracewell Hill (in front of the White Bear) on the right are a number of new apartments and these stand on the site of a row of mid-nineteenth century buildings that incorporated the Co-op rooms (later to become AIN Chemicals), the Temperance Hall and three houses higher up. These have now all gone and the oldest building here is Green Bank Farm. This was once part of the Charles Farm estate and the people listed as farmers in the earlier days of the White Bear Inn farmed this area.

Pasture Gate Farm

Where Pasture Lane once carried straight up the hill stands the building of Pasture Gate Farm – this was commonly known as *'The Piece House'* suggesting that a trade in woven wool or cotton pieces was carried on here. This was the home of the Butterfield family for many years during the later nineteenth century – the same family who farmed at Oaklands Home Farm in the early years of the twentieth century and who gave their name to Butterfield Street. *Pasture Gate* was the name of Pasture Lane when it was a small dirt track serving the farms of Green Bank, West Pasture, Pasture House and Spittlefield Head.

Lower Fulshaw Farm

To the west on the heights of Pasture Lane are a few scattered small farmsteads, the largest of these being Higher Fulshaw which stands alongside the ancient east-west ridgeway. Lower down the ridge slopes, in 1847, were the Royal Oak Cottages, two Lower Fulshaw Farms and Lower Fold. The main reason for the siting of these farms and houses was the large area of sheep pasture that had been taken into cultivation here in the sixteenth century. The smaller farms were built by the wealthier woollen merchants of the district who supplied raw wool to the market and manufactured woollen cloth.

Perhaps the earliest extant building of the type erected by the new breed of merchant in the Fulshaw area (the Old English *ful = cleared* and *shaw = woodland*) is that of Lower Fulshaw. This is a three-cell house of two storeys with a stone over the doorway showing the date of 1630. The doorway itself sports a heavy ogee head with a heavily-chamfered surround and the downstairs windows have hood mouldings with carved label stops. Lower Fulshaw was probably built by Bernard Sutcliffe, yeoman, who had a son also named Bernard (d. 1674) - in the 1630s the Sutcliffes of Fulshaw were recorded as having 31½ acres of land. Bernard junior's death predated that of his father and this meant that his sister, Margaret (d. 1722), inherited Lower Fulshaw. Margaret married Henry Rycroft and he carried on his business as a farmer and wool merchant at Fulshaw. When Henry died in 1709-10 his will showed that he had 2 looms in his shop and was owed the sum of £279: 5s: 3d for wool by 16 different people. He also had 30 pack sheets and this suggests that he was a clothier as well as a woollen merchant. One of Henry's debtors was William

Roberts, another woollen merchant from Hollin Bank in Marsden, who owed the Rycroft estate £17. This family eventually ended up farming at Lower Fulshaw in the nineteenth century.

Lower Fulshaw Window Hood Moulding

Carved Label Stops

Former original doorway used for loading wool and cloth into the loom shop (early 17th c)

Lower Fulshaw was variously known as Fulshaw, Pasture and Rycrofts Farm - in the 1660s the house was listed as having two hearths. It appears that Bernard Sutcliffe would have been a tenant of Lawrence Towneley of Stonedge in Blacko as, in 1635, Towneley owned *'Fulshaw and the pasture lands.'* This could well have been a reference to the main farm of Higher Fulshaw which, in 1539, was occupied by James Hartley. In 1549 Hartley was involved with other tenants of Barrowford in a law suit against Henry Bannister, of Park Hill, and others to enforce them to *'keep a sufficient way'* between the Alms Kiln at Whittycroft and Admergill. In 1567 Christopher Smith of Fulshaw was appointed overseer of Barrowford township and in 1567 Christopher Robinson was summonsed because his; *'Hedges at Fulshaw are left open where they adjoin the land of Bernard Hartley of Lawnde'* (Collings Clough).

In the second half of the eighteenth century William Hanson of Roughlee owned the extended Fulshaw area and his three daughters married James Lord, John Robinson and John Hartley thus allowing them inheritance of the Lower Fulshaw lands. In 1800 James Hartley of Higher Fulshaw, a calico manufacturer, entered into an agreement with a number of other local manufacturers to *'set a caul and direct Barrowford water at Reddyford Myll.'* This was a reference to the creation of a mill lodge behind what would become the site of Holmefield Mills. This lodge provided water and power to Reedyford Mill (or Hodge Bank Mill) that stood beneath the spiral walk-way spanning the M65 motorway from Scotland Road to Reedyford Road. In 1825 probate of Christopher Hanson's will (son of William) left his farm in Roughlee to Thomas Grimshaw and James Hartley in trust for his daughters who had married James Holt, James Robinson and Thomas Rawson and the remainder of his property to his son William Hanson.

In 1831 James Hartley, of Higher Fulshaw, and Thomas Grimshaw, of Higherford, sold 8 acres of the Hanson farm in Roughlee: *'Closes called the Holme, the Great and Little Hive Banks, the Lower and Higher Parts of the Old Meadow and the Haycroft, in Roughlee Booth,'* to William Baldwin and in 1835 James Hartley is described as a land valuer of Fulshaw. In the later nineteenth century Lower Fulshaw had been swallowed up by the Parker-Holt-Swinglehurst estate of Park Hill, all of which was offered for sale as separate farms in 1921.

The Lower Fulshaw Doorway
The date stone above says BS 1630

The head moulding is reminiscent of Pearsons Farm at Wycoller (c.1680).The unusual layout of the house was rare locally but more common over the border in Yorkshire

James Hartley (70) was still at Higher Fulshaw in 1841 along with his wife Alice (60) and their family while son John Hartley (55) was also farming here with 3 housekeepers and 1 agricultural labourer. At Lower Fulshaw in 1841 were four separate families:- James Holt (35) with 2 children, 2 women workers and 1 agricultural labourer:- James Holt

(54), a farmer of 35 acres with daughter Marie and Sarah Bradshaw (dairy maid):- Margaret Roberts (45), farmer with her son and his wife and their 3 daughters (all handloom cotton weavers):- Richard Roberts (25), a farmer with his wife Betty (20) and son John (1 month):- Henry Roberts (44), a farmer of 20 acres with 3 children and 1 orphan child.

In 1861 we find John Hartley (55) farming 42 acres at Higher Fulshaw with his 3 sisters and a nephew. At Lower Fulshaw were Henry Roberts (44), a farmer of 20 acres with his sister, a niece, a grandson and an orphan child: James Holt (54), a farmer of 35 acres with daughter Marie and Susan Bradshaw (dairy maid) – the marriage of this James Holt to the daughter of Christopher Hanson brought one of the Lower Fulshaw farms into the Holt family and this is why it would become part of the Holt estate at Park Hill. In 1871 Henry Roberts (55) was a farmer of 21 acres at the *'Lower Fulshaw Farm House'* along with sister Betty (57) and son James (17). Maria Hartley (71) is now farming 42 acres at Higher Fulshaw with her sister Jane (58), sister Margaret and nephew George Hartley (27), an agricultural labourer.

Ten years later George Hartley (37) was a farmer of 65 acres at Fulshaw Height along with his wife Mary Jane (28) from Grassington and their son James (3 months). Working on the farm are Stephen Towler (21), a farmer's assistant from Skipton, Jane Hartley (68 - George's aunt) and Margaret Hartley (61 - his mother). At Lower Fulshaw in 1881 were Henry Roberts (64), a farmer of 21 acres and his sister Betty (66). William Walton (44), of Barrowford, is shown to be a *'hired farmer'* at Lower Fulshaw with his wife Eunice (43) and 3 sons Richard (17), James (6) and William (4). In a cottage at Lower Fulshaw at this time were William Bowker (38), a night watchman from Grassingham, his wife Ellen (33), from Barrowford, son William (6), daughter Alice Ann (4), son Ashworth (2) and son John (8 months). In 1935 a descendant of this family, Thomas Bowker of Gisburn Road, died from food poisoning when an outbreak affected 30 people in Barrowford, the source was thought to have been tainted boiled ham.

In 1896 Stephen Towler farmed Lower Fulshaw and in 1846 the farmers here were Harold Lancashire and Willis Lowcock; today it is owned by Philip Hanson whose family have been here for many years.

Many of the photographs within this book have been kindly supplied by Mr. R J Hayhurst. Without the foresight of historians who saw the long-term benefits to our society in the saving of records, both photographic and written, then books such as this would not be possible.

Photographs:

The R. J. Hayhurst Collection
The late Albert Morris Collection
The late Jim Sanderson collection
Roderick Gregg
Nelson Leader
Nelson Library (Local Studies)
Colne Library (Local Studies)
Stanley Graham
Others: J A Clayton

Sources:

Blakey, J. *Annals and Stories of Barrowford* 1929
Doreen Crowther – unpublished papers Nelson Library
Gladys Whittaker – unpublished papers Nelson Library
Farrer's *Clitheroe Court Rolls* Vols I-III Colne Library
Barrowford Almanac series (courtesy of R Gregg)
Lancashire Records Office, Preston
Miller, E. M. J. *A Walk Though Barrowford* 1983
Nelson Leader
Leeds Mercury
Melanie Whitehead (Sutcliffe material)
Pearson, S. *Rural Houses of the Lancashire Pennines* 1985
Published BMD records – Newchurch-in-Pendle and Colne
Shackleton, G. *The Textile Mills of Pendle* 2006
Various deeds, indentures etc. held by the author
Yorkshire Archaeological Society
Mike Rothwell – *Industrial Heritage* 2006
Dennis Green & Doreen Crowther research – *A Bannister Family History* Heritage Trust NW 2006

Other Titles by the Same Author

Valley of the Drawn Sword *Early History of Burnley, Pendle and West Craven*   ISBN 978-0-9553821-0-9 2006

The Lancashire Witch Conspiracy (1ST and 2nd editions) *A History of Pendle Forest and the Lancashire Witch Trials* ISBN 978-0-9553821-2-3 2007

Rolling Out the Days (editor) *From a Barrowford childhood to wartime Burma*   ISBN 978-0-9553821-3-0 2007

Cotton and Cold Blood *A True Story of Victorian Life and Death in East Lancashire*   ISBN 978-0-9553821-4-7 2008

Admergill with Blacko and Brogden *History and Archaeology of an Ancient Pennine Estate*   ISBN 978-0-9553821-6-1 2009

Local History Series - **Lower Barrowford** 978-0-9553821-5-4 2009 **Central Barrowford** 978-0-9553821-7-8 2009
Higher Barrowford 978-0-9553821-8-5 2010 **Blacko** 978-0-9570043-0-6 2011

The Pendle Witch Fourth Centenary Handbook   *History and Archaeology of a 1612 Landscape*   ISBN 978-0-9553821-9-2   2012

The Other Pendle Witches   *The Pendle Witch Trials of 1634* ISBN 978-0-9570043-2-0   2012

The Annals and Stories of Barrowford *(Republication of Blakey, J. 1929)* ISBN 978-0-9570043-1-3   2013

Burnley and Pendle Archaeology - Part One *Ice Age to the Early Bronze Age*   ISBN 978-0-9570043-3-7   2014

Burnley and Pendle Archaeology - Part Two *Middle Bronze Age to Iron Age*   ISBN 978-0-9570043-3-7   2014